The POWER *of*
CONSECRATION

The POWER of CONSECRATION

A Prophetic Word to the Church

JEREMIAH JOHNSON

DESTINY IMAGE® PUBLISHERS, INC.
P.O. Box 310, Shippensburg, PA 17257-0310
"Promoting Inspired Lives."

This book and all other Destiny Image and Destiny Image Fiction books are available at Christian bookstores and distributors worldwide.

Cover design by Esther Eunjoo Jun
Interior design by Terry Clifton

For more information on foreign distributors, call 717-532-3040.
Reach us on the Internet: www.destinyimage.com.

ISBN 13 TP: 978-0-7684-5078-1
ISBN 13 eBook: 978-0-7684-5079-8
ISBN 13 HC: 978-0-7684-5081-1
ISBN 13 LP: 978-0-7684-5080-4

For Worldwide Distribution, Printed in the U.S.A.
4 5 6 7 8 / 23 22 21 20

DEDICATION

I dedicate this book to the precious Holy Spirit. Thank you for your commitment to sanctify us through and through. I agree with your declaration! *"May your whole spirit, soul and body be kept blameless at the coming of our Lord Jesus Christ"* (1 Thess. 5:23).

ACKNOWLEDGMENTS

I want to thank Dr. Annette Graves for helping me birth the final pieces of this manuscript. Your kind words and encouragement much like a midwife were just what I needed. Thank you for your hours of research and editing. We share the same heart for the Consecrated Bride. Maranatha, Come Lord Jesus!!!

Finally, thank you to my precious wife and four children. I love you with all of my heart and I'm so grateful for the gifts that each of you are to me. Thank you for teaching me the power of consecration even at home and doing life together. The work of the Holy Spirit is so evident in our lives. May we be ready for when our Bridegroom King returns!

CONTENTS

FOREWORD

YEARS AGO I WROTE A LITTLE BOOKLET CALLED *Nazirite DNA*. It was the message that fueled 20 years of the ministry of "TheCall," a movement that gathered hundreds of thousands to fast and pray for revival and reformation in individual lives, families, and nations. The book was a call to affection-based consecration to God. Not legalism but love. Not "I have to" or "I should have" but "I get to" for the sake of love and for divine encounter and reward.

I read the book you are now reading by Jeremiah Johnson in one sitting. The book has been calling me back

1

to my original DNA. The book has searched the shadows of my soul, haunted me if you will, wooing me back to a fresh grace filled crisis of consecration to that single hearted love for Jesus which is the wellspring of all true happiness. Simply put, my friend Jeremiah Johnson has written one of the best and most important books on consecration I've ever read. It is a true trumpet call to my own heart and I think to a whole generation that is saturated with pleasures and entertainments beyond our wildest imaginations. That saturation will be the foundation to a great apostasy and/or the testing ground out of which the Bride of Christ will arise victorious to love her bridegroom Jesus with such singular intensity as to magnetize His second coming, culminating in the wedding of Christ and the Church.

Forty-three years ago as a youth pastor I went into that Methodist church late at night to pray. Kneeling at that altar in the sanctuary I cried to God, saying, "God, as a boy who grew up in church, if You can't make me as radical and as intense a lover of God as a drug addict who got radically saved and has a testimony of complete deliverance, then I don't want to follow You." Then and there I made the words of that old hymn the lifelong prayer of my heart, "Spirit of God descend upon my heart, wean it from earth through all its pulses move. Stoop to my weakness, mighty as Thou art, and help me love You as I ought to love. Teach me to love You as Thine angels love, one holy passion filling all my frame, the baptism of the heaven-descended dove, my heart an altar and Thy love the flame." *One holy passion.* What a searching word. Only one passion?

And the Man to whom I prayed that prayer, the Man whose name is Jealous, has ever since been the Hound of Heaven to my heart, ever stalking me with love, searching my inward affections, and seeking to drive out all those false suitors who promise but can never fill the pleasure center of my soul. I was made for God alone and complete consecration to Him is the only true highway to the extreme pleasures of His Presence.

And oh how I have been tested and often fled from the pursuing Presence. How I have often sought solace in lesser pleasures, shrinking from the altar of sacrifice upon which only the fire of love falls.

The whole life of Abraham, the friend of God, could be boiled down to consecration choices and tests of love, whereby every divine subtraction leads to divine multiplication and heavenly pleasure (reward). God is always cutting away that which hinders pure love and always giving us back something of Himself far beyond. "Take now thy son, thine only son, and offer him up on the mountain I show you." "I swear, because you have not withheld your son, your only son whom you love, I swear your children will be like the stars of the sky and the sand of the seashore."

I once penned this simple poem that describes the tests in my own life to consecrate my soul to this one holy passion: "How hard it is to part with Isaac. He is deeply rooted in my soul, but just call my name and I'll say here I am, like Abraham, I want to be a covenant man." That has been easier said than done, but to the degree I've submitted to the knife of God's love—to that degree I've found fire.

Jeremiah Johnson in this book quotes John Piper, "We easily deceive ourselves that we love God unless our love for Him is frequently put to the test, and we must show our preferences not merely in word but with sacrifice."

I grew up listening to Dodgers baseball on the radio with my father. What fun! I love the Dodgers right fielder Cody Bellinger. He is on a hitting and fielding tear at the time of this writing. I love to watch the videos of Clayton Kershaw and Bellinger over and over again. What a wonderful pleasure. But when I ongoingly wake up in the morning and the first thing I want to do is open up my Dodgers baseball app, it is then I hear the footsteps of my Jesus walking in the cool of the garden of my heart whispering, "Where are you, Lou? How easily we drift from the fire of devotion into the lukewarm love of a lax, cultural Christianity.

I can hear the voices of those reading this last paragraph crying "legalism!" But really? I know it. You know it. I know when a series of novels eats me up with desire to read and the hungry spirit within me cries "feed me!" But no bread from heaven is given. We cannot sing about God's fire all the while knowing that fire is all consuming. The gospel of grace is way too sharp a sword than we've allowed to wound us. Let's let our semi- complacent souls and convenient grace boxes allow for a little disturbance. This book is a disturbance to self-satisfied religionists. But it's a biblical disturbance and one that has motivated me by grace to press on to the prize if the high calling of Christ.

Oh, and the chapter on bridal fasting is worth the whole book. I'm realizing that the fast Jesus spoke about when the bridegroom is absent is as all-consuming and intense as John the Baptist's fast who was the friend of the Bridegroom. Should not the Bride long for His return more than His friend? Jesus declares that this fast is the God-given channel for such longing. Feasting in the joy of the Holy Spirit in the New Covenant is paradoxically connected with the groaning and longing for Jesus's Presence here, now, and for His second coming. Feasting is ever linked with joy and fasting is linked with longing. We get to participate in both in this present dispensation.

Reading this book I found the preciousness of the sweet pain of longing stirring up within me again. The Church must rediscover the groan for fullness. It's the paradox of "the already" and the "not yet." Here in this book we see the plight of the prophet. The prophet always sees the fullness of Christ and through his fasting and prayers and proclamation groans in a fresh revelation of Christ. Then when everyone is rejoicing in the new manifestation the prophet sees again and is again groaning for the "more." What's a prophet to do? Jeremiah is that kind of prophet. He has encountered God and encountering Him calls the people to a fresh consecration so they too may encounter.

At times Jeremiah has been to me that "oh troubler of Israel." But in reality he has troubled my compromised heart. When you read this book, seek not to judge the man but let the message judge your manner of life. Heed this call to bridal consecration and let the cross be the crossover into a life crowned with passion and power.

Lou Engle

INTRODUCTION

ECENTLY, I'VE HAD TWO PASSAGES RESTING ON ME IN a deep way: Matthew 9:14-15 and Revelation 22:17. In Matthew 9, the disciples of John come to Jesus and ask the question, "Why do we and the Pharisees fast often but You and Your disciples do not fast?" The question they are asking is why when it comes to consecration, spiritual discipline, and holiness we are more dedicated, disciplined, and consecrated than You and Your disciples. Jesus answers their question with a question: "Can the friends of the bridegroom mourn as long as the bridegroom is with them? But the days will come when the bridegroom will be taken away from them, and then they will fast."

Jesus's answer to their question is, in my opinion, the very crux of Jesus's mission to produce holy, consecrated people. Jesus in essence is telling them, "I have one agenda for these three and a half years and that is addicting them to My Presence, My nearness, and My words. These friends of the bridegroom are being ruined over Me and they are developing a taste for Me. The days are coming when I will be taken away from them, and when I'm taken away from them they will be cut to the heart, and from that moment all of their consecration, spiritual disciplines, and holiness will not be a religious duty to get My attention but will be the response of a someone ruined and sick with love. They will simply miss Me and want Me more than anything or anyone else."

"Then they will fast." Can you feel Jesus's confidence? Can you feel the heart of the Bridegroom God? Our God is a Bridegroom. He didn't come for religious system but for a Bride wholly set apart unto Him because she has settled it: "His love is better than wine. His love is better than anything this world can offer." Friend, have you encountered the intoxicating love of our Bridegroom? The Bride that comes into this revelation will be so dangerous. She will be so much more than having outward forms of religiosity but will burn on the inside with holy, violent love for the Son of God.

This is the new wineskin that Jesus came to release on the earth, and it's this new wineskin that will be able to contain the new wine of the glory of the Lord. Jesus tells us that He is not going to put the new wine of His glory into old ways and old definitions of consecration, holiness, and spiritual disciplines but is first going to establish the new paradigm in His people and it will be this new paradigm that will be able to steward the new wine of His Presence.

I'm convinced that Jesus is also speaking of corporate structures in the Church. He is declaring that the structures that will be useful for end time glory and shaking will be ones that are sick with love for the Bridegroom. The Church that will prioritize mourning for Him and His Presence and put that wound at the center will be the one that will be entrusted with apostolic government, resources, and influence. He isn't going to entrust last-days authority to churches who are more interested in cleaning the outside of the cup while never letting the fire of His Spirit address religious harshness, lawlessness, lust, and the greed of the inside of the cup.

We are in the middle of a wineskin change—the body of Christ and our understanding of consecration at the center of it. This is all I'm hearing from the Spirit of God in these days. I'm feeling it personally, corporately, and globally.

"The Spirit and the Bride say come!" One of the last verses in the Bible declares what we will look like before He returns. In this verse, we see a Church in unity with the Holy Spirit, a Church operating in a bridal paradigm, and we see a Church anointed with the Spirit of prayer. God will use great glory and great shaking, great Presence and great pressure to produce a great prayer. The baptism of fire is coming to the Church to clean the inside of the cup and place the seal of fire on the heart of His bride. The fire of the Holy Spirit will bring forth capability in His people from the inside out, and she will come into unity with Him and each other, and she will radiate His glory and holiness. She will be adorned with righteousness. She will shine. And she will want Him more than anything else.

Right now, it's a whisper, but I hear it getting louder and louder.

In *The Power of Consecration,* Jeremiah Johnson sounds a clarion call to the body of Christ of this exact paradigm shift that is taking place regarding consecration, holiness, and spiritual disciplines. *This* is the core issue, and we cannot afford to dismiss it. If we do, I'm afraid we will be unable to steward all that God is doing in these last days and He will pass us by.

I've loved all of Jeremiah's books and messages, but I would say the message of this book is touching some of the deepest things in the heart of God. I wholeheartedly endorse this message and pray that God will cause it run swiftly across the globe and prepare us for our wedding day.

COREY RUSSELL
Author and speaker

CHAPTER ONE

THE PROPHETIC WORD TO THE CHURCH

For the last ten years, I have been primarily teaching the body of Christ in the USA and parts of the world the specific subject matter of consecration. The need for consecration burns in me like a fresh fire shut up in my bones. The honest truth is that in many circles, the very reason why I am even invited to come speak and minister is because the church or conference host knows that I love to preach on this specific subject found in the Word of God.

With this background and some years of experience in mind, I sat down to write this book believing that with hundreds of sermons and hours' worth of notes, I could easily lay out a very clear path to the power of consecration and what God was saying to the Church. My, how wrong I was!

I quickly realized that God was actually inviting me into a fresh encounter concerning the power of consecration and that I needed to put quite a bit more prayer and fasting into writing this book. Through many tears and fresh revelation, I suddenly realized that I have been teaching the power of consecration with limited understanding! I myself needed a serious upgrade before I could share God's heart concerning this subject.

As I began to dialogue with God about what He wanted to say to us, I was made aware that more than diving into the mechanics of what it looks like to be fully consecrated unto Him, He wanted to reveal the "why" behind this subject matter. In other words, why consecrate ourselves as believers?

Again, I admit that this was a unique question and journey for me personally because as I have been preaching and teaching holiness and consecration all over the world for a focused period of time, I have honestly never considered this question. I have certainly labored to preach on clear biblical standards for holiness and also our biblical identity of who we are in Christ. But never have I taught a message on "why" we should give ourselves to being a consecrated people. Could there actually be more than just telling people to be holy because God is holy?

I suddenly began to wonder if I had actually missed preaching the eternal storyline that links our personal and present commitment to consecration to the future and ultimate day where we shall be fully consecrated before our Bridegroom King? Sadly and with great tears, I confess that I have. However, I believe this is why I have written this book and why God now wants to release a prophetic word to His Church. Here is what He spoke to my heart in the place of prayer over this manuscript:

"For many years, My Bride has sought to consecrate herself before Me without My eternal storyline in mind. They have sought to fast, pray, and separate themselves from the world with only present hopes and desires of revival and awakening. However, in this generation I am releasing the 'why' behind the 'what': namely the Wedding Day. See, I am releasing a revelation of My pure and spotless Bride that will stand before Me one day so that My people might not grow weary and lose heart on their journey to become like Me. While a present focus on personal holiness and consecration will only last for a time, a vision of the Wedding Day will be the power behind My consecrated ones in the days ahead. There is a love-sickness that shall come upon My Bride that will give Her doves' eyes. Pure and simple devotion to Me will be the mark of a consecrated people that will stand before Me."

As God whispered this prophetic word to my heart on the power of consecration, I wept and wept. He began to say to me over and over again in the secret place, "And the Bride shall make herself ready."

CHAPTER TWO

THE BRIDE HAS MADE HERSELF READY

I N REVELATION 19, WE SEE THE BREATHTAKING AND beautiful marriage supper of the Lamb with the first corporate gathering of the saints of old and the generation in which the Lord returns. John the Apostle writes and says, *"Let us rejoice and be glad and give the glory to Him, for the marriage of the Lamb has come and His bride has made herself ready"* (v.7).

Imagine all of heaven is gathered, the Lamb of God, our Bridegroom King and Judge is present, and the very first thing that we agree and rejoice in as the Bride is Jesus Christ judging the harlot Babylon. We need to pause and digest that tremendous reality. As the Bride of Christ, gathered on the wedding day, I repeat, the very first thing we will do is corporately rejoice and agree in Jesus Christ judging Babylon for her immorality and martyring the saints (Rev. 19:1-8).

When John writes that the *"bride has made herself ready,"* he is describing more than an outward appearance and radiance on the wedding day, but also an inward revelation and intimate knowledge of who our Bridegroom King really is. The Bride is going to wholeheartedly embrace and even rejoice at every action and decision

Jesus Christ makes, including His judgements of harlot Babylon, the nations, and people who reject Him.

Unfortunately, we are living in a day and age where too many in the Church are being deceived concerning who Jesus Christ really is and especially His judgements. The words of Jesus Himself in Matthew 24:10 ring painfully true describing His own return when he says, *"And then many will be offended, will betray one another, and will hate one another."*

THE LION OF JUDAH APPEARS

I have recently had a series of prophetic encounters that led to the Lord Jesus Christ appearing to me for the third time in my life, clothed in white garments with fire in His eyes. The holy fear, trembling, awe and pure wonder totally consumed me and was the same experience I had with Him in the two encounters before. His sheer beauty is terrifying, and His Presence takes your breath away. The light that radiates from His being is so pure that you become more aware of your great need of Him than ever before.

I will never forget our conversation in that specific encounter. I do not take lightly or treat these encounters haphazardly. Anyone who claims to have actually seen and interacted with our risen Lord needs to carry a serious fear of who He really is and an undeniable mandate on their life to make Him known. This is not a joke. It's very weighty and does not involve vain imaginations. As the Lord Jesus Christ appeared to me, He said, *"Jeremiah, many know the Lamb who went to Calvary, but few know the Lion who is returning to devour His Father's enemies. The same wrath that was poured out on the cross will be the same wrath that will be poured out in judgment upon my return."*

He continued, *"I am releasing apostolic and prophetic messengers who will trumpet my end-time judgments to the Church and warn of the consequences of those who only know the Lamb of mercy and grace, but reject the Lion of judgment and wrath. Many only know Me as the great intercessor, which I am, but I am also the coming King and judge. There is more than intercessory prayer. For I will teach My people in these last days how to pray kingly and judicial prayers. I will establish My government in the earth and make My enemies a footstool. I will rule and reign with an iron scepter."*

I began to shake and He said, "Jeremiah, many will be offended at My return! They have created a god in their own likeness and image and will deny Me when I come with all My glory, power and splendor! You must warn the Church of the scoffing spirit that will come, of the overemphasis of My goodness and never teaching on My severity, of never proclaiming and warning of My wrath and judgment that is here now and is yet to come."

The look in the Lord Jesus Christ's eyes as He said these words to me was so intense, yet so deeply grieved. He then asked me if He could entrust me with these words, and I said yes. When I did, He turned around and vanished from my bedroom. I shook for days and have never recovered.

THE POWER OF CONSECRATION

As we begin to dive into the call to consecration and all that God wants to speak to the Church, we must understand that the power of our consecration is found in our personal revelation of who Jesus Christ really is. Ultimately, our lifestyle choices are a direct reflection of who God is to us. If we as the Bride of Christ are going to have consecrated ourselves for the Wedding Day in Revelation 19,.then we must make it an absolute priority to see and know Jesus Christ for who He really is. God is releasing a revelation of the Lion of Judah to the end-time Church to help us get ready for His return. God is raising up apostolic and prophetic messengers who will trumpet the end-time judgments of God to the Church and warn of the consequences of those who only know the Lamb of mercy and grace, but reject the Lion of judgment and wrath.

A PROPHETIC WARNING

Be on the lookout for one of the greatest end time delusions and deceptions of our time: the denial and attempts at erasing the judgments of God from the New Covenant. Beware of false apostles, prophets, and teachers who will convince the saints that the judgments of God are cruel and unjust. The real Bride of Christ will arise and agree and rejoice in His Judgments! Beware of those who will falsely declare that Jesus Christ has already returned again. It is a lie from the pit of hell.

A Personal Invitation

I want to invite you now as the reader, to get into the place of prayer and ask yourself, "Am I preparing and consecrating myself now for the Wedding Day? Do I realize that the present day call to consecration is directly connected to our future presentation before our Bridegroom King? Will I be offended because I only know Jesus as the Lamb and do not see Him as the Lion? Do I have an issue with His end-time judgements?"

Remember, the power of our consecration will ultimately be revealed in our revelation of who Jesus Christ really is.

CHAPTER THREE

THE CONSECRATED BRIDE

IN THE MIDST OF A TREMENDOUS AND DARK ASSAULT upon this generation, God is gathering a Consecrated Bride who will be completely devoted to His Son Jesus. In Hebrew, the word *qadash*, used 172 times in the Old Testament, means "set apart." It is translated into English as "consecration." Paul urges believers in Second Corinthians 6:17 to "Come out from them and be separate... Touch no unclean thing and I will receive you."

The call to be consecrated, to be set apart, living holy and separated unto the Lord, weaves its way throughout the Old and New Testament. In Revelation 18, immediately before the Wedding Day of the Lamb and His Bride, John hears a voice from heaven that tells believers "Come out of her, my people, so that you will not participate in her sins and receive of her plagues."

Clearly, the invitation to consecration has a solid foundation in the Word of God. In fact, it is a command.

THE DARKNESS AND GLORY OF GOD

Isaiah foresaw and prophesied about the evil trying to overtake our nations when he declared "darkness will cover the earth and deep darkness the people." But he didn't stop there. "The Lord rises upon you," he continued, "and His glory appears over you" (60:1-2).

A Consecrated Bride is beginning to emerge out of the present darkness covering the earth. She is rising still. Many of these sons and daughters are invisible now, but they will be invincible in the days ahead, clothed with the radiant light of God! As darkness increases in the nations of the earth, the Consecrated Bride will receive Isaiah's words that now is the time for Her to arise and shine!

The Consecrated Bride recognizes that the darkest hours are before the dawn. The increase of evil does not discourage her or make her fearful.

Is the world's darkness strong?

Yes.

But that is not the question facing the Bride.

The question the Church must ask and commit herself to answer is this: *How strong and how bright is the light that is coming?*

According to Proverbs 4:18, "the path of the righteous is like the light of dawn that shines brighter and brighter until the full day!"

The light that is shining and will shine in the days ahead is going to be absolutely spectacular! This brilliant, beautiful light will shine through the Consecrated Bride as She separates herself, purifies herself, and reflects the glory of God.

Consequently, a massive awakening and revival will move through the nations of the earth.

CONSECRATION AND DEMONSTRATION

During the darkest and most turbulent days in Israel's history, God raised up consecrated individuals like Samson, Samuel, and John the Baptist to shake His People out of complacency and confront idolatry in the land. These men were known as "Nazarites" because of their radical devotion to Yahweh. Their commitment to deny themselves the legitimate pleasures of this life so that they might experience a greater measure of satisfaction in God set them apart from the rest of their generations.

A radical consecration born out of encountering the jealous love of God in the same spirit of the Nazarites is our only hope in this current hour. The lack of demonstrations of the power of God in the Church now is directly linked to our lack of consecration.

God is going to pour out His Spirit without measure to a Consecrated Bride who chooses to live outside the spiritual mixtures of this world.

CONSECRATION IS NOT LEGALISM

Do not be surprised, however, when many in the Church begin to label the call to consecration as legalism simply because they have never encountered the true power and deliverance that the love of Christ brings.

The answer to a compromised world is a Consecrated Bride filled with fiery love for her Bridegroom King. The call to consecration was also despised and rejected in the days of Amos.

He records the attack: "I also raised up prophets from among your sons and Nazarites from among your men. But you made the Nazarites drink wine and commanded the prophets not to prophesy" (Amos 2:11-13).

God's people demanded that the prophet Isaiah "stop confronting us with the Holy One of Israel!" (Isa. 30:11).

One of the primary reasons why the Consecrated Bride will be attacked and persecuted is because of the lukewarmness She will expose in the carnal church. Her passion, devotion, and love will challenge the status quo and continually call the saints into deeper encounters of intimacy with their Bridegroom King.

We must be on the lookout for targeted attacks against individuals and churches full of love and passion for Jesus. The joy they find in Jesus and the sacrifices they are willing to make out of their devotion to Him will generate jealousy, insecurity, and accusation in those whose walks are less committed.

A WARNING TO THE CONSECRATED BRIDE

I cannot overemphasize that being a Consecrated Bride is more than maintaining an outward appearance of purity and devotion. The Nazarites of old grew their hair long to represent their inward devotion to God, but the Consecrated Bride of today and the future will be known by Her inward-burning heart. Nothing less than intimate encounter with Jesus Christ consecrates these ones and compels them to make significant sacrifices for the Kingdom of God.

Mike Bickle, founder of the International House of Prayer warns the Bride of what could happen if She focuses on outward behavior modification instead of inviting the Spirit of God to change her first on the inside:

> The danger of Nazarite consecration is to be holy on the outside, but inwardly carry a hard and self-righteous heart that hides behind the mask of righteousness and impressive outward actions that disguise a bankrupt soul.

> Only the fire of inward intimacy, the filling of the Holy Spirit along with continuously receiving God's mercy and delight for us, even when

we fail, can deliver us from the Pharisaical heart. Nazarites who are not living in intimacy with the Lord also face the danger of self-righteousness when they rejoice in their commitment to Jesus and not in Jesus Himself.[1]

A PROPHETIC DREAM

In a season of crying out to the Lord for the DNA that would mark the Consecrated Bride, God gave me a dream in which Mike Bickle, Lou Engle, and Corey Russell gathered together.

In the dream, each man wore a T-shirt. Mike Bickle's T-shirt read "Shulamite"; Lou Engle's T-shirt said "Nazarite"; and Corey Russell's T-shirt proclaimed "Nasharite."

God immediately spoke to me in the dream and said, "The Consecrated Bride that is emerging in the earth will possess this three-chord strand that cannot easily be broken. The Shulamite anointing represents love and intimacy, the Nazarite anointing represents consecration and holiness, and the Nasharite anointing represents prayer and fasting."

"The DNA of the Consecrated Bride must be the marrying of intimacy, consecration, and prayer. It is out of those three realities that My Kingdom will be displayed in fullness and power in the days ahead."

The Shulamite, Nazarite, and Nasharite

The Shulamite Bride in the Song of Solomon asks Solomon to "Kiss me with the kisses of your mouth, for you love is better than wine" (1:2).

In other words, the Shulamite anointing resting upon the Consecrated Bride will crave intimacy with Jesus over anything else the world has to offer because She has experienced a realm of encounter with Him that she cannot find anywhere on earth. A realm of lovesickness and romance unlike anything we have known before is going to rest upon the Church in the last days. Songs, sermons, and prophecies will be released that directly involve the wooing, longing, and aching of the Bride for her Bridegroom King to come.

The Nazarite calling had three vows attached to it: the cutting of the hair, drinking wine, and being around the dead were forbidden according to the law. The fire fueling this restrained lifestyle was measured in the heart behind these choices. The Consecrated Bride will choose to abstain from many pleasures that the world offers in pursuit of a higher pleasure: the Presence and Person of the Bridegroom King.

The Nasharite anointing comes from a man named Daniel Nash. At the beginning of the Second Great Awakening in America, Daniel Nash, at 48 years of age, gave himself totally to pray for the meetings of revivalist Charles Finney.

Nash would enter towns and cities weeks before Finney's scheduled awakening meetings and travail in the place of intercession and prayer that God might pour out His Spirit upon the meetings.

Once Nash entered a city and found only a dark cellar to pray ahead of time. Lying prostrate on the ground and groaning, he called on the name of the Lord and pulled heaven to earth.

When Finney would arrive and begin the awakening meetings, Nash typically did not attend. He would continue praying in secret for souls and deliverance.

Several hundred thousand souls were brought into the Kingdom during the Second Great Awakening.

Nash died in 1831. His gravestone reads:

DANIEL NASH

Laborer with Finney

Mighty in Prayer

Nov. 17, 1775–Dec. 20, 1831

Nasharites are voices of deep prophetic intercession that shift regions and nations as they release the words and heart of God through prayer and fasting. Just as Daniel Nash committed himself as a voice of prophetic intercession, giving time and resources to the place of travail before Charles Finney, the messenger of awakening, would preach, even so God is releasing this anointing in the earth.

This Nasharite army in the earth will win heaven's blessing and approval before revival and awakening meetings occur in cities and regions.

It is this colorful, vibrant, prophetic vision and brilliant description of the Consecrated Bride that will cause Jesus, our Bridegroom King, to declare at the end of the age: "Arise and get ready now, for the marriage supper of the Lamb has come and the Bride has made Herself ready."

May we continue to understand that the power of our present commitment to consecration is fueled by this glorious picture of our Wedding Day.

Our Bridegroom King is declaring over us, "You have ravished my heart, my sister, my bride, you have ravished my heart with one glance of your eyes" (Song of Sol. 4:9).

NOTE

1. Mike Bickle, *Jesus Fast*.

CHAPTER FOUR

THE HARLOT BRIDE

DURING THE WRITING OF THIS BOOK, I HAD A prophetic dream where I saw the table of contents. This chapter had been left out and the voice of the Holy Spirit clearly said to me, "In the last days, there will be two dueling Brides that will rise in the earth: The Consecrated Bride and the Harlot Bride. The Consecrated Bride will marry itself to the Bridegroom King; the Man of War and the Harlot Bride will marry itself to the world and look like Babylon."

As a result of this supernatural encounter, I have dialogued with the Holy Spirit and written this chapter with urgency and a special burden knowing God Himself wants this subject addressed.

As I woke up from the prophetic dream deeply troubled, I asked the Holy Spirit to be very specific regarding what the Harlot Bride will look like in the earth so the Consecrated Bride can be warned. He gave me five specific attributes regarding her. They are:

- Sexual Immorality

- Drunkenness

- Tolerance

- Greed

- Pride

James reveals the core of the Harlot Bride when he writes, "You adulteress, do you not know that friendship with the world is hostility toward God. Therefore, whoever wishes to be a friend of the world makes himself an enemy of God" (4:5).

Very simply put, the Harlot Bride loves the world and enjoys friendship with it. The Consecrated Bride is in love with the Bridegroom and develops special friendship with the Holy Spirit.

DIVING DEEPER

In Revelation 18, "Babylon" is described as having fallen before the Wedding Day: "And she has become a dwelling place of demons and a prison of every unclean spirit, and a prison of every unclean and hateful bird. For all the nations have drunk of the wine of the passion of her immorality, and the kings of the earth have committed acts of immorality with her, and the merchants of the earth have become rich by the wealth of her sensuality" (18:2-3).

In the prophetic dream, the Holy Spirit specifically said to me, "The Harlot Bride will marry itself to the world and look like Babylon." In Revelation 18, I believe the Harlot Babylon represents the systems of the world.

Therefore the Harlot Bride will be heavily involved and participating in worldly systems.

John warns, "Do not love the world, nor the things of the world. If anyone loves the world, the love of the Father is not in him. For all that is in the world, the lust of the flesh, and the lust of the eyes and the boastful pride of life, is not from the Father, but is from the world" (1 John 2:15).

Let's take a closer look at the five attributes of the Harlot Bride.

SEXUAL IMMORALITY

A good-looking young adult couple recently approached me at an altar asking for a prophetic word of blessing regarding their relationship. Expecting me to just quickly bless them, they bowed their heads immediately.

Without even seeking the Lord, I said, "Are you two sleeping together?"

The look on their faces as their heads snapped up was priceless. There was no need for an answer.

"You are asking me to bless something that the Word of God has clearly already called sinful," I told them. "You don't need a prophetic word. What you need to do is repent of your sins, stop sleeping together, separate, and then I'll pray God's blessings upon you." They marched out of that church faster than I could blink and gave me the middle finger on the way out the door.

To be completely transparent, as I continue to preach across the United States and globally every year, I'm fully convinced that if the true uncompromised gospel of Jesus Christ was boldly preached with authority in many of our churches, they would be emptied out rather than filled up. God is releasing bold prophetic messengers in this hour that will specifically confront the sin of sexual immorality in the Church and raise up a standard of righteousness in the land

Sexual immorality is at the top of almost every list of sins in the New Testament. It is emphasized in the book of Revelation as one of Satan's primary weapons against the Church in the end times (Rev. 2:20; 9:21; 14:8; 17:1-4).

If someone is continually and habitually engaging in sexual immorality and calling themselves a Christian, they are deceived (Rom. 6).

Lifting our hands up on Sunday morning and pulling our pants down on Friday night is not okay. Heterosexual, homosexual, bi-sexual, and however else sexual you want to get, but if it's not in covenant as defined by the Word, then God doesn't bless it. He condemns it.

It doesn't matter if someone attends a supernatural school of ministry, speaks in tongues and prophesies, their daddy's a preacher, or their under some false grace teaching. If we are not saving ourselves for marriage, we are selling ourselves to the devil!

DRUNKENNESS

The Harlot bride will have a very casual approach to drinking alcohol and this will cause many would-be Nazarites to stumble and fall. Amos indicts the spirit of harlotry in leadership: "You made the Nazarites drink wine" (Amos 2:12).

There is a steady pressure and worldly culture that has infiltrated much of the Church that welcomes casual drinking and even drunkenness. Paul warns in Ephesians 5:18, "Do not get drunk on wine, which leads to debauchery. Instead, be filled with the Spirit!"

TOLERANCE

The Harlot Bride will be tolerant of many ways to heaven and will not be clear on her stance toward righteousness and consecration. She will welcome various sexual orientations and provide a safe place for all sorts of perversions to worship together.

GREED

The Harlot Bride will be governed by her love of money. She will sacrifice the truth of the gospel for pleasure and entertainment. The Harlot Bride's leaders will fleece the sheep and be continually hungry for monetary gain.

Revelation 18:3 says, "[T]he merchants of the earth have become rich by the wealth of her sensuality."

PRIDE

The worst attribute of the Harlot Bride will be her pride. The Harlot Bride will glory in her perversion and harlotry. She will mock the Consecrated Bride and persecute those who walk in humility and meekness. Revelation 18:7 says of her that, "To the degree she glorified herself... to the same degree give her torment and mourning."

FINAL WARNING

Speaking of the Harlot Bride who will marry herself to the world and look like Babylon, God says, "Come out of her, my people, that you may not participate in her sins and that you may not receive her plagues" (Rev. 18:4).

If you are reading this chapter and find yourself engaged in sexual immorality or casual drinking that leads to drunkenness, or you sense you are full of pride or a lover of money, you still have time to repent. If you find yourself thinking that all world religions provide a way to God and you do not feel the exclusive call of Jesus Christ to salvation, you still have time to repent.

If the Holy Spirit is weighing heavily upon your mind and heart right now, turn to Him and surrender these sins at the foot of the Cross. You are called to be the

Consecrated Bride, not the Harlot Bride. In the generation in which the Lord Jesus Christ returns, we can expect two dueling brides to rise in the earth.

BECOME A FRIEND OF THE BRIDEGROOM

Keep your eyes open for the emergence of friends of the bridegroom in the earth carrying a specific mandate to confront and remove the spot and wrinkle from the Harlot Bride prior to the return of the Bridegroom. These prophetic voices will be like hot irons from the fire. They will press out and apply great pressure to anything and everything that is unclean and defiled.

They will be oracles of righteousness, friends of the bridegroom gripped by repentance and the fear of the Lord, prophets who despise and weep over wickedness and sin. They are forerunners, deliverers, and faithful to the truth no matter what it costs them.

Their convictions are fierce; their consecration is intense. Everyone else wants to tone them down and moderate their crying out.

These friends of the bridegroom are Nazarites: pure ones, separated unto God with great seasons of prayer and fasting.

They sing one octave too high for the religious.

They are functioning to prepare the Bride to meet the Bridegroom. They have been branded by the reality of the "pure and spotless" Bride. They are called to be a Consecrated Bride. They will be confrontational and appear harsh and radical in the eye of the casual Christian, but they will be mighty end time oracles in the hands of Almighty God!

They groan for the glory of God to be fully manifested in the Bride and they understand that this can never happen until wickedness and sin is confronted. Let these friends of the bridegroom arise! Oh, how we desperately need them in these days!

"Blessed are those who wash their robes, that they may have the right to the tree of life and may go through the gates into the city. Outside are the dogs, those who practice magic arts, the sexually immoral, the murderers, the idolaters and everyone who loves and practices falsehood" (Rev. 22:14-15).

CHAPTER FIVE

THE GIFT IS IN THE GROAN

J ESUS IS RELEASING A GROAN IN THE EARTH. AN ACHE, a longing, an unquestionable thirst and heart cry for His return.

He has given his Bride this groan as a gift to keep our hearts and spirits awake when they are prone to sleeping. He is inviting us to embrace the tension of living between his first and second comings!

There are deep questions that we have to consider as the Consecrated Bride if we are going to steward this incredible gift of groaning. Are we willing to remain in the vulnerability of hunger at the heart level for years, continuing in the way of lovesickness even when disillusionment comes knocking on our door and the fire of when we first got saved seems too extravagant and too extreme?

What about when the options set in, the responsibilities rise, the children come, and the cares increase?

Will we fight for the simplicity of loving Jesus radically and press against the torrential wave that carries away so many from whole-hearted consecration over the course of years?

When decades turn and years accumulate, will our lives be such that Jesus would say over our later years that love found its victory in us, and the steady tide of love became a mighty wave that no longer needed prodding but swept us effortlessly in its strength?

Oh, that love would abound and win over us, burning within us in such a way that it does not diminish over decades but steadily increases until the day we see His face?

In his book *Systematic Theology*, Wayne Gruden puts it this way:

"Do Christians in fact eagerly long for Christ's return? The more Christians are caught up in enjoying the good things of this life and the more they neglect genuine Christian community and deep intimacy with Jesus, the less they will long for his return. To some extent then, the degree to which we actually groan for Christ's return is a measure of the spiritual condition of our lives right now."[1]

"I want to deliberately encourage this mighty groan for Jesus!" A. W. Tozer wrote.

> The lack of it has brought us to our present low estate. The stiff and wooden quality about our religious lives is a result of our lack of holy desire. Complacency is a deadly foe of all spiritual growth.

Acute desire must be present or there will be no manifestation of Christ to His people. He waits to be wanted.

Too bad that with many of us He waits so long, so very long, in vain.

O God, I have tasted Your goodness; it has both satisfied me and made me thirsty for more.

I am painfully conscious of my need for more grace—and I'm ashamed of my lack of desire for His return.[2]

Tension in the Believer

As born-again believers in Jesus Christ, we all feel this tension.

Peter calls it "the war against your soul" (1 Pet. 2:11).

Paul tells us we feel this tension because we live in "this present evil age" (Gal. 1:4).

Because we truly love Jesus, this present delay suspends our hearts and souls in a radical and inescapable tension.

We don't fit in! We are in the world but not of the world? We don't manage our sin; we live in freedom and deliverance. So many of us settle for "normal" Christianity because we have no understanding of the revelation that we are created for eternal glory!

To minister to the Lord and enjoy His pleasures that can only be found in His Presence!

We miss out on nothing in the world, Beloved. They are missing out on what is going on here!

Why don't we fit into the world's standards?

Jesus tells us it is because the world hates Him. "If the world hates you, know that it has hated me before it hated you. If you were of the world, the world would love you as its own; but because you are not of the world, but I chose you out of the world, therefore the world hates you" (John 15:18-19). Those who are in Christ—who belong to Him—are not of the world, "just as I am not of the world" (John 17:16).

Paul stresses this relationship, warning us that "many... walk as enemies of the cross of Christ. Their end is destruction, their god is their belly, and they glory in their shame, with minds set on earthly things," but reassuring us that "our citizenship is in heaven, and from it we await a Savior, the Lord Jesus Christ" (Phil. 3:18-20).

"These all died in faith, not having received the things promised, but having seen them and greeted them from afar, and having acknowledged that they were strangers and exiles on the earth," the writer of Hebrews describes our heroes of the faith in Chapter 11. "For people who speak thus make it clear that they are seeking a homeland. If they had been thinking of that land from which they had gone out, they would have had opportunity to return. But as it is, they desire a better country, that is, a heavenly one. Therefore God is not ashamed to be called their God, for he has prepared for them a city."

When Peter warns us of the war against our souls, he calls us "sojourners and exiles" (1 Pet. 2:11).

This world is not our home!

Jesus blessed our hunger in Luke 6:21: "Blessed are you who hunger now, for you shall be filled." He knew our human propensity to allow our hearts to become stifled and captured by a thousand lesser loves.

He knew that without this hunger and aching after God, our hearts would become content with the temporary fixes that give us pleasure, even though momentary.

THE GIFT IS IN THE GROAN

Living between the two comings of Christ means that one part of us stretches back in faith, love, and remembrance of His first coming while the other part stretches forward in expectant hope, desperate longing, and loving desire for His second coming.

Jesus describes this tension as a perpetual mourning for Him, the Bridegroom. This mourning is the inevitable suffering of soul in which His friends would live when He was no longer with them. He alluded to this when His disciples asked him why they were not fasting like John the Baptist's disciples. Jesus answered, "Can the wedding guests mourn as long as the bridegroom is with them? The days will come when the bridegroom is taken away from them, and then they will fast" (Matt. 9:14-15).

Jesus assumed that we would mourn for him when He was gone and that we would fast in His absence out of our deep desire for His return!

When was the last time we fasted for the return of Jesus because we were sick of the world we live in and the absence of the Kingdom of God's full manifestation on earth?

To understand this mourning, we must grasp how radically Jesus's Presence touched His disciples' lives.

They would ache, they would groan for his return after He had been taken from them!

I imagine Jesus in these moments looking at the disciples and knowing after He left that they would never again be able to live as they had done before.

Love had had its way in them!

He had not come to earth to visit them; He had come to walk with them!

And being around Jesus had ruined them for anything less than the continued experience of being near Him.

In the days to follow, how great would be the sufferings of their hearts! The sufferings of all who loved Him and called Him friend on earth. The power and potency of their memories and their experiences with Him would cause an incessant groan to remain unanswered until they could see His face again and be with Him once more.

Jesus understood his absence would initiate an inner groaning, a love pang for Him that would fuel every sacrifice and empower ever service for the rest of their earthly lives.

On the eve of His departure He was preparing them for this future: "Let not your hearts be troubled. Believe in God; believe also in me. In my Father's house are many rooms. If it were not so, would I have told you that I go to prepare a place for you? And if I go and prepare a place for you, I will come again and will take you to myself, that where I am you may be also. And you know the way to where I am going" (John 14:1-4).

Thomas was troubled by Jesus's words. "Lord, we do not know where You are going. How can we know the way?" he asked.

"I am the way, and the truth, and the life. No one comes to the Father except through me," Jesus responded (John 14:5-6).

This was the Father's heart plan from the very beginning. Jesus would so wound the hearts of His friends in love that motivated by their desire for His Presence and wrenching ache for Him and His return, they would pour out their lives upon Him rather than waste their time on the pleasures of the earth.

They were so radically impacted and changed by their encounter with Jesus, they willingly died for Him!

Some of us have been so unaffected by our relationship with Christ that we can hardly give him a Sunday morning.

We can find it difficult to connect to God's storyline, but it is a love story. Jesus Christ came to the earth, turned twelve fishermen into lovesick disciples, paid with His life a debt they (and we) could not pay, went to the grave, rose again, and is coming back as our Bridegroom in jealous love for His Bride.

We are that Bride. We are going to have to cry out, "Maranatha! Come Lord Jesus!"

"The Spirit and the Bride say, 'Come!'"

"Things are not okay when you are not with us!"

The days we are living in between His first and second comings are not meant for our disillusionment but are ordained for a harvest of souls and for the Bride of Christ to become pure and spotless. This delay is intended to create a desperate groan, ache, longing, and desire for Him throughout the earth.

Jesus wants the culmination of all our passion and desire for Him and His second coming to manifest as living blamelessly in holy love before Him.

John Piper puts it like this: "The Bridegroom left on a journey just before the wedding, and the Bride cannot act as if things are normal. If she loses him, she will ache for his return."[3]

The Consecrated Bride will refuse to be comforted by the things of this world because She has been given the Holy Spirit as a free taste, a down payment, a guarantee of the fullness of relational Presence with Jesus that is to come!

Have you ever received a letter form a loved one so far away that, while their words brought great comfort, yet they afflicted your heart with a painful longing for them?

This is called the Divine Wounding.

The Holy Spirit confronts us with the indwelling Presence of Jesus Christ while simultaneously spawning a yearning for the fullness of finally seeing him face to face.

Paul expresses it this way. "For in this tent we groan," he shares, "longing to put on our heavenly dwelling, if indeed by putting it on we may not be found naked. For while we are still in this tent, we groan, being burdened—not that we would be unclothed, but that we would be further clothed, so that what is mortal may be swallowed up by life. He who has prepared us for this very thing is God, who has given us the Spirit as a guarantee. So we are always of good courage. We know that while we are at home in the body we are away from the Lord, for we walk by faith, not by sight" (2 Cor. 5:2-7).

And Jesus returns this groan. "Father, I desire that they also, whom you have given me, may be with me where I am," He prays, "to see my glory that you have given me because you loved me before the foundation of the world" (John 17:24).

Though He is in us by His Spirit, Jesus cried out for His full inheritance: that all whom the Father gave Him would be with Him where He is.

We live now as those betrothed to a Bridegroom, anticipating a real wedding.

THE DILEMMA

Though our minds know that Jesus Christ came two thousand years ago, died, and rose again, and our mouths confess to being His Bride, awaiting his return, the longing, ache, and groan in our hearts for him is disproportionate to the times we live in.

The difficulty is this: though we claim deep love for Jesus, the degree of our satisfaction in the way things are indicates otherwise. If we really love Jesus, why do we not groan and ache for Him in His absence?

Could it be that our lack of groaning and crying out for His return could be significantly tied to our lack of truly knowing Him?

What husband loves his wife and yet lives undisturbed and untroubled if she is taken from him?

Wayne Gruden sums up our dilemma: "To some extent, the degree to which we actually groan for Christ's return is a measure of the spiritual condition of our lives right now."[4]

Are we groaning for His return today? Are we feeding the ache of the Holy Spirit within us for the fullness of Jesus, or are we busy snuffing and starving the groan by being drunk on the busyness of life and our desire for this world's pleasures?

Jesus is looking for a lovesick Bride willing to lay everything down out of her passionate desire for Him.

The gift of the groan is not given to make our lives more difficult. The gift of the groan keeps our hearts awake when they are inclined to sleep.

The inner groan keeps our hearts in love for God. It keeps us hungry to know Him and the power of His resurrection and the fellowship of His sufferings (Phil. 3:10).

The gift of the groan keeps us reaching for eternity so that we might live free of the deception of the lusts of this age and the comforts of the temporary. Will you receive the gift of the groan today?

NOTES

1.   Wayne Gruden, *Systematic Theology*, Grand Rapids, MI: Zondervan, 1994, p. 255

2.   A. W. Tozer, *The Pursuit of God*, n.p.

3.   John Piper, *A Hunger for God*, Wheaton, IL: Crossway Books, 1997, p. 86.

4.   Wayne Gruden, *Systematic Theology*, Grand Rapids, MI: Zondervan, 1994, p. 178

CHAPTER SIX

A NEW KIND
OF FASTING

I N MATTHEW 9:14-15, THE DISCIPLES OF JOHN THE Baptist approach Jesus and ask, "Why do we and the Pharisees fast, but your disciples do not fast?" Jesus responds to them by saying, "The attendants of the bridegroom cannot mourn as long as the bridegroom is with them, can they? But the days will come when the bridegroom is taken away from them, and then they will fast."

When Jesus walked the earth, fasting was associated with mourning. It was an expression of sorrow, desperation, and brokenness typically over sin. People disciplined themselves to fast when things were not going well for them. Jesus's response to John's disciples is shocking and full of revelation!

In essence, Jesus is communicating to them that His Presence on earth with His disciples was so glorious that His disciples had no need to fast!

He then proceeds to compare His arrival on earth to the coming of a bridegroom to a wedding feast.

Listen closely.

"BUT the days will come when the bridegroom is taken away from them, and THEN they will fast" (9:15).

Jesus was not nullifying fasting; He was emphasizing to the disciples of John that while He walked the earth it was a time of celebration and rejoicing. He would eventually leave and then it would be time to enter into a new kind of fast.

Jesus explains in verses 16-17: "But no one puts a patch of unshrunk cloth on an old garment; for the patch pulls away from the garment, and a worse tear results. Nor do men put new wine into old wineskins; otherwise the wineskins burst, and the wine pours out, and the wineskins are ruined; but they put new wine into fresh wine skins, and both are preserved."

The accustomed type of fasting was no longer suitable for the new reality of Jesus's Presence and the Kingdom He was establishing on earth. The unshrunk cloth and the new wine represented the fresh reality that had come with Jesus. The new type of fasting He was unveiling is built upon the mystery that the Bridegroom has come, and that that He will come again!

The paradox inherent in this new kind of fasting is that, in Jesus, the desired Kingdom was present with them, but that it would come in greater measure in the future on His return.

In Luke 17:21, Jesus tells His disciples that "the kingdom is within you," but in Luke 22:18, He explains to them that He "will not drink from the fruit of the vine until the kingdom of God comes" (speaking of His future return).

Jesus so profoundly yet simply tells all those who have an ear to hear that the new kind of fasting he is introducing to His followers is not fasting from a place of emptiness, mourning, and sin, but learning to fast from the place of being IN HIM and longing and aching for more of His fullness.

OUT WITH THE OLD

After participating in and leading numerous kinds of fasts most of my Christian life, I am absolutely convinced by experience that most Christians fast with the mindset and understanding of the disciples of John. Fasting to these individuals seems to be some type of last resort and/or yearly routine that they use to dig themselves out of lethargy, spiritual complacency, and sometimes sin. Their attitude and heart is bent toward sorrow, desperation, and, at times, self-condemnation. But what about this new kind of fasting Jesus is introducing to the disciples in Matthew 9:14-17?

I believe the Consecrated Bride rising in the earth will not only participate in this new kind of fasting, but lead in calling her members to the fast. The invitation will be simple: Come and learn how to fast from the place of tasting and seeing that God is good and aching and longing for more of where that came from! The Consecrated Bride is going to fast because She is so lovesick for her Bridegroom King, she cannot eat.

The groaning, aching, and longing for the return of Jesus Christ driving this Bride to fast will not be an expression of emptiness. This new kind of fasting will be born out of her current encounter with the wine of Christ's Presence and her yearning for more!

This new kind of fasting is hunger for fullness. It is stirred out of experiencing the pleasures that can only be found in the Presence of Jesus and the aching for that day when we meet our Bridegroom face to face.

This new kind of fasting is, in fact, feasting upon Jesus himself and groaning for the Wedding Day when we will dine and rule with Him forever from the Wedding Table of the Lamb!

A LIFESTYLE OF FASTING

Jesus told the disciples of John that fasting would be necessary when He left until He returns again.

In Matthew 6:16-18, He frames fasting in such a way that His expectations are clear: if you are one of His disciples, then you will fast. It's not a matter of *if* you should fast, but *when* you will fast.

But why fast?

Let's take this new kind of fasting a step further. What is Jesus after when He calls the Consecrated Bride to participate in a lifestyle of fasting?

John Piper puts it this way: "We easily deceive ourselves that we love God unless our love for Him is frequently put to the test and we must show our preferences not merely with words but with sacrifice!"[1]

Fasting has the express capability of exposing deception. We may think that we are more in love with Jesus Christ than we really are. Fasting food, entertainment, and other gifts from Above has the power to drop a plumb line in our lives and show us where we are crooked and in need of straightening.

Fasting increases our hunger for God. It fuels our desires for a deeper encounter at His table. It reveals how many masters we are serving (1 Cor. 6:12).

Fasting crucifies our flesh. As God tells me every time I visit the Garden of Gethsemane in Israel, "If you do not crucify your flesh privately, your flesh will crucify you publicly."

THE ENEMIES OF THE CONSECRATED BRIDE

Jesus came to earth and handed the disciples in Matthew 9:14-17 a great weapon. He has given the Consecrated Bride the gift of a new kind of fasting to prevent her from becoming a Harlot Bride.

Without a lifestyle of fasting, we cannot cultivate the kind of hunger and extravagant desire for Jesus that he is so worthy of.

"If we do not feel strong desires for more of God," John Piper points out, "it is not because we have experienced him and are deeply satisfied. It is because we have worshipped the gifts he has given us for so long. We have stuffed ourselves with small things and have no real appetite for God things."[2]

God is constantly inviting us into a deeper experience of Himself and if we are to cultivate our love for Him, we must make significant sacrifices. The most dangerous enemies of the Consecrated Bride are not necessarily the evils of this life but the good gifts God has given us. The pleasures of this life and our desires for good things can all become deadly substitutes for God.

The Consecrated Bride is going to dine at the Bridegroom's table of encounter, for the table of the world has nothing to offer her any longer. A new kind of fasting is a powerful weapon in the Consecrated Bride's arsenal to keep her hungry, aching, longing, and lovesick for her Bridegroom King. God is an inexhaustible fountain and is ready to serve an infinite feast to all those who are willing to forsake the legitimate pleasures of this life in order to inherit a higher degree of satisfaction in Him.

There is a seat available right now at His table of encounter. Will you respond in love?

NOTES

1. John Piper, "Awakening Your Appetite for God," *Life Action*, Life Action Ministries, 8 April 2016.

2. John Piper, *A Hunger for God: Desiring God through Fasting and Prayer,* Wheaton, IL: Crossway, 2013, p. 71.

CHAPTER SEVEN

THE TABLE OF ENCOUNTER

IN REVELATION 19:9, JOHN THE BELOVED WRITES about a special feast between the Bridegroom and Bride when he says "Blessed are those who are invited to the marriage supper of the Lamb."

Indeed, the invitation to come and dine at our Bridegroom's table of encounter is an extraordinary one. We are given a foretaste by Jesus Himself about the cost of sitting at this table when He tells a story in Luke 14:16-24.

Jesus says, "A certain man was giving a big dinner, and he invited many; and at the dinner hour he sent his slave to say to those who had been invited, 'Come; for everything is ready now.' But they all alike began to make excuses. The first one said to him, 'I have bought a piece of land and I need to go out and look at it; please consider me excused.' And another one said, 'I have bought five yoke of oxen, and I am going to try them out; please consider me excused.' And another one said, "I have married a wife, and for that reason I cannot come.'"

GOING DEEP IN GOD

The Holy Spirit constantly and continually invites us to journey deeper into the mysteries of God (1 Cor. 2). Jesus specifically says in this parable, "Come, for everything is ready now." But His kindness is quickly rejected by dinner guests with numerous excuses. If I could summarize their mistake (and often times our own), it would simply be this: We will always reject God's invitation to journey deeper into His heart so long as we lack or have an incomplete revelation of who He is and what He has provided for us at His table of encounter.

One of the foundational principles of the Kkingdom of God is built upon the revelation that the deeper we go in Jesus, the less we can take with us. As we experience His love, our excuses, schedules, and plans become insignificant as we encounter a higher degree of Presence and learn to abide in Him.

I was a really busy young man until I met my wife. As soon as she showed interest in developing a relationship with me, my calendar suddenly cleared and I was excited and enthusiastic about courting her. What exactly changed in my life? I began to experience a deeper degree of love and affection with her that trumped everything else in my life.

Many Christians hear the invitation to go deeper in God, to consecrate themselves further, to separate from the things of this world, and many of them just can't seem to get there. Why?

I believe it is simply because they do not have a revelation of who has invited them to the table of encounter and all that Jesus Christ has prepared at that table for those who love Him. King David testified of the power of spending time in God's Presence as he wrote and said of the Lord, "You have made known to me the path of life. In your Presence is fullness of joy, in your right hand there are pleasures forevermore" (Ps. 16:11).

J. I. Packer, in his book *God Has Spoken*, says this about God's purposes for revealing Himself to us: "[God's purpose]... is to make friends with us. It was to this end that He created us rational beings, bearing His image, able to think, hear, speak, and love. He wanted there to be genuine personal affection and friendship, two-sided between Himself and us."[1]

THE THREE EXCUSES

What stopped the wedding guests from responding to Jesus's invitation to the table of encounter? Pondering their excuses provides us a window of revelation that we cannot afford to miss if we are to be prepared for the marriage supper of the Lamb in the days ahead.

The dinner guests made three excuses for why they were not present at that table: (1) a piece of land, (2) five yoke of oxen, and (3) a wife.

What is so evil about a piece of land, five yoke of oxen, and a wife?

The answer is profound: NOTHING!

There was nothing inherently evil about their excuses. That issue opens a revelation to us as Jesus's Consecrated Bride that we desperately need in this generation!

As we go deeper in God and journey into the depths of who He is, He no longer just comes after our sin stuff. He actually requires the good stuff!

When the message of repentance and consecration goes forth in most churches, many Christians are checking off their religious lists to make sure they haven't committed any "big" sins that are keeping them from going deeper in God. In this parable, Jesus is actually laying out profound revelation to the Consecrated Bride who will dine at His table of encounter and the marriage supper of the Lamb!

He is declaring, "There is a realm of encountering Me and understanding the fruit of My rewards that will swallow up all our excuses. The good gifts that I have given you just cannot be turned into gods any longer."

This is a real paradigm shift for the Consecrated Bride. We are no longer just allowing the Holy Spirit to convict us of the sin that separates us from God; we are constantly and continually sacrificing the good things of this life in order to enjoy the legitimate pleasures of heaven.

Bill Johnson puts it this way: "Many Christians repent enough to get to heaven, but few people repent enough to experience heaven on earth."

In other words, how deep are we willing to allow the Holy Spirit to search us so that we might experience all that God has prepared for us on this earth?

THE FRUITS AND ROOTS

As I have come to the revelation and understanding from Luke 14 that our level of encounter is determining our level of surrender, my approach and response to the message of consecration has completely changed. In fact, I realized as a preacher that I had often addressed the fruits of people's disobedience (their excuses) without ever getting to their core issues: the roots of their disobedience.

"If you love Me," Jesus says in John 14:15, "you will obey My commands."

In other words, it is a loving encounter with Jesus Christ that truly produces the obedience and surrender that He is worthy of. For years, I would preach hard against sin and confront Christians' excuses of why they weren't serving God without ever inviting them into an intimate encounter with the Son of Man! Again, the old religious spirit in me would say that our level of surrender is determining our level of encounter.

I realized through Jesus's revelation of Luke 14 that the only way to sustain a lifestyle of consecration is deep intimacy with our Bridegroom King.

Encountering Jesus

Loving God is the highest priority in the Kingdom and the greatest way to live. When asked about the greatest commandment in the Law, Jesus puts it this way: "You shall love the Lord your God with all your heart and with all your soul and with all your mind. This is the great and first commandment. And a second is like it: You shall love your neighbor as yourself" (Matt. 22:35-39).

Jesus commands wholehearted obedience, yet invites us into a red hot love affair with Him. When we attempt to obey God apart from intimacy with Him, we model ourselves after the Pharisees and our obedience is motivated by religious legalism. If we ever find ourselves in a place of abiding in Him without obeying His commands, we have fallen into hyper grace theology that will eventually lead into wickedness and sin. Thus the goal and ultimate desire of the Consecrated Bride should be obedience that is fueled from intimacy.

THE THREE STAGES OF LOVE

The Father is looking for wholehearted obedience and devotion, both personally and corporately, but our ability to do that hinges on our crying out for the revelation of who He is in fresh encounters with His love and affection for us.

The motivations and thoughts of the believer's heart are revealed through three different types or stages of obedience. "Fear-based" or "shame-based" obedience flows from the fear of being shamed by inadequate performance or the suffering of negative consequences. This obedience is biblical, but such motivations will not enable us to consistently resist the pleasures of sin over a lifetime of temptations.

Duty-based obedience is obedience that acts but does not feel God's Presence in the actions. God's Word requires that we obey God even when we do not feel inspired to do so or feel His Presence in the actions.

This type of obedience is also biblical.

Affection-based obedience is obedience that flows out of our encounters with Jesus's love for us and moves us to love him in return. This kind of obedience has the power to keep us from temptations over a lifetime. A lovesick person will endure and sacrifice anything for the one they love.

Can you hear and feel Jesus our Bridegroom King inviting you and I as His Consecrated Bride to His Wedding Feast? The table of encounter is being set even now for the end of the age. Great sacrifice and the deepest levels of consecration we have ever known will be required in order to sit at His table, yet the secret and overwhelming desire of our God is obedience fueled out of intimacy with

Him. As Jesus said to me one day, "Jeremiah, you must obey me because I'm your King, but I want you to fall in love with Me because I'm also your Bridegroom." May our levels and depths of encounters with Him only increase exponentially in the days ahead!

NOTE

1.   J. I. Packer, *God Has Spoken*, Baker Academic; 3 edition (May 1, 1994) page 72.

CHAPTER EIGHT

DROP THE PLUMB LINE

GOD IS DOING SOME ABSOLUTELY SPECTACULAR things in this generation because many have dared to agree with Jesus and declare, "Your Kingdom come, Your will be done on earth as it is in heaven" (Matt. 6:8-10). Much of the Church is truly discovering the realities of heaven and asking God to establish them by His grace on the earth.

I have had the privilege and opportunity to minister the gospel and prophesy in more than 40 states in the USA and over 25 foreign nations around the world. I have witnessed a tremendous increase of the miraculous as well as significant moves of the Holy Spirit. A stirring to pray and seek the face of God like never before is touching numerous churches and ministries throughout the world.

For example, we know that there is no sickness and disease in heaven (Rev 21:4). Therefore, as this generation is praying "on earth as it is in heaven," we are seeing an outbreak of signs, wonders, and miracles like never before. We also know that in heaven there are twenty-four elders and four living creatures surrounding the throne of God who are worshipping and praying around the clock (Rev. 4:6-7). As this generation dares to pray, "On earth as it is in heaven," we now have more houses of prayer being raised up in the earth than at any other time in history! How wonderful!

However, with the increase of the supernatural and special emphasis on prayer and worship in these days, both of which are heavenly realities, I would like to boldly suggest that we have forgotten a third primary reality in heaven that holds the key to a powerful three-cord strand in this generation that will not be broken. It's called the key of holiness and consecration!

Have we forgotten the words that the twenty-four elders and four living creatures are forever and continually crying out before the throne of God? They are declaring, "HOLY, HOLY, HOLY is the Lord God Almighty who was and who is to come."

The supernatural plus prayer/fasting/worship plus consecration equals the Kingdom of God on earth as it is in heaven!

While this generation has dared to pray, "On earth as it is in heaven" (verse 10), we have forgotten to include verse 9, which says, "Our Father in heaven, hallowed be Thy Name."

The proper translation is actually this: "God, Make Your Name Holy." When I married these two verses together, I began to experience the power that is contained within the words of Jesus. Listen to them closely:

DROP THE PLUMB LINE

"God, make Your Name holy, Your Kingdom come, Your will be done, On earth as it is in heaven."

My experience testifies that the call to consecration is the missing link in this generation.

THE LOST ART OF CONSECRATION

Traveling and ministering around the USA and the world, I have experienced many movements and churches who absolutely welcome the supernatural along with prayer and worship.

But the moment I start preaching and teaching on holiness and consecration, the air gets sucked out of the room. I have cried out to the Lord with much weeping on many occasions and said, "God, how is it possible that so many love miracles, prophecy, prayer, and worship, but they do not want to hear about Your holiness? Why do conferences fill up when we advertise the miraculous, worship, and prophecy, but hardly anyone attends if we start addressing character and integrity?"

Several years ago, I was a part of a conference leadership team where we were ministering on the gifts of the Holy Spirit. The conference registration sold out and the first night was off the charts. There was a strong prophetic flow and signs, wonders, and miracles broke out. We worshipped for over two hours. At the end of the meeting, we announced that the next night we would be talking about living a lifestyle of consecration and the sacrifices that it takes to go deeper into God's heart.

To our amazement, only 25 of the conference attendees showed up the next night.

Only 25 percent!

At the end of that night, we announced that the following night we would be doing more miracles and prophecy. What happened? The building was packed out with standing room only!

In other words, we have a charismatic generation addicted to the supernatural, but allergic to the word of God!

I want to be clear; this is not an isolated incident. I have witnessed this pattern all over the USA and the world!

I believe we have a charismatic generation who embraces the supernatural power of God—giftings, prophecy, evangelization, prayer, worship, miracles— but the moment holiness and consecration is mentioned, everyone flees! How terrifying! I consistently meet Christians around the world who are ready to lay hands on the sick, but they can't keep their hands off a boyfriend or girlfriend.

We have a generation of worship leaders who don't care if the musicians and singers are saved, let alone living holy before God. We just want to pay professionals for their skills on a stage when we should be dropping a plumb line and raising up a standard of righteousness in the Church. Perhaps the greatest earmark of a generation chasing the supernatural with no biblical foundation is the fact that they categorically reject the message of repentance and wholeheartedly embrace various so called forms of "love" that embraces people in their sin, but fails to call them out of it.

REVIVAL HISTORY

With a generation so desperate for revival and awakening, the power of consecration is absolutely necessary to see heaven come to earth. We must continue to pray for the miraculous and engage in prayer and worship, but the call to holiness and consecration must not and cannot be ignored any longer.

Loren Sandford, commenting on the history of revival in the Church, says, "Every past revival in Christian history has been based on a foundational cultural agreement concerning right and wrong, sin and morality. When society departed from that foundation, everyone knew it. As a result, people could respond to great preaching, feel guilt over their sin, turn to God and repent. Revival grew and spread on the basis of repentance and the forgiveness that flows from the cross and the blood, in large part because everyone understood the baseline from which they had departed and to which they could return. No such cultural agreement now exists. Even in much of the contemporary

Church we have lost the sense of sin and with it, any need to repent. Without a sense of sin, repentance cannot come, and without repentance, revival in the fullest sense can never happen."[1]

There has been a continual and systematic erasing of a baseline or plumb line in our generation. The truth is that our lifestyle choices are either highlighting or erasing a clear standard of holiness and righteousness in the land. Moral relativism denies absolute truth and leaves what is right and wrong conduct up to however we feel. We must reject this deception. Moral absolutism says there is a clear standard of what it means to be consecrated and there are right and wrong ways of doing things. The standard determines what is right and wrong.

Sexual immorality is at the top of almost every list of sins in the New Testament. It is emphasized in the book of Revelation as one of Satan's primary weapons against the Church in the end times (Rev. 2:20; 9:21; 14:8; 17:1-4).

If someone is continually and habitually engaging in sexual immorality and calling themselves a Christian, they are deceived (Rom. 6).

Lifting our hands up on Sunday morning and pulling our pants down on Friday night is not okay. Heterosexual, homosexual, bi-sexual, and however else sexual you want to get, but if it's not in covenant as defined by the Word, then God doesn't bless it. He condemns it.

It doesn't matter if someone attends a supernatural school of ministry, speaks in tongues and prophesies, their daddy's a preacher, or their under some false grace teaching. If we are not saving ourselves for marriage, we are selling ourselves to the devil! How can we be so zealous in this generation to lay hands on the sick and prophesy when we can't even keep our hands and mouth off our boyfriend/girlfriend?

The plumb line must be dropped on this issue in America and the nations of the earth! Let a standard of righteousness and holiness be clearly marked in our lives and in our church communities. Without holiness, the Church has nothing to say to the world.

The Call to Consecration

Without consecration, the Church has nothing to say to the world. God wants to give this generation encounters like those experienced by Israel, encounters that caused them to call Him "the Holy One of Israel." Light and darkness were colliding in the days of Amos. God encounters Amos beside a vertical wall with a plumb line in His hand and asks Amos, "What do you see?"

"I see a plumb line," replies Amos.

"Behold, I am about to put a plumb line in the midst of My people Israel and I will spare them no longer!" the Lord declares (Amos 7:7).

The Lord uses the plumb line symbolically to refer to the divine standard against which God, the builder of His people, tests and judges them.

It also symbolizes the standards by which God will rebuild His people.

"So shall they fear the name of the Lord from the west, and his glory from the rising of the sun; When the enemy comes in like a flood, the Spirit of God shall lift up a standard against him," proclaims Isaiah (59:19).

THE GREATEST CALLING OF ALL TIME

I, like you, have listened to many (if not hundreds) of Christians tell their stories of when they were "called."

Called into the ministry at youth camp. Called to the mission field as a married couple. Called to adopt; called to finance etc.

Christians respond to all sorts of callings. But the greatest call on the life of a Christian is one that I have never heard anyone share.

Peter tells us that God has called us to be holy. "But just as He who called you is holy, so be holy in all you do, for it is written: 'Be holy because I am holy.'" (1 Pet. 1:15-16).

In Romans 1:7 and First Corinthians 1:2, Paul greets believers in Rome and Corinth as those "called to be holy."

He tells the Thessalonians that God did not call them to be impure, "but to live a holy life" (1 Thess. 4:3-8).

Paul underscores this later in First Thessalonians when he says, "The God of peace sanctify you through and through," adding "The one who calls you is faithful and He will do it" (5:23-24).

We have not only been called to be holy and live holy as believers, but this has been the plan of God for our lives from the beginning of time!

"He chose us in Him before the foundation of the world [to] be holy and blameless before Him," Paul tells us in Ephesians 1:4.

To know and understand what God has called us to is of infinite importance. Christians complaining of an absence of joy and strength in their lives, of failure of will and lack of happiness, have not embraced the call to holiness.

How many more deceived Christians are going to divorce because they aren't happy when that has never been the primary purpose of marriage in the first place? Holiness is the purpose of marriage. Happiness in marriage is a by-product of giving ourselves to holiness and seeing our spouse as an instrument in the hand of the Lord to perfect us.

Paul uses marriage as a picture of God's work of sanctification in our lives, exhorting husband to love their wives as Christ loves His Church "having cleansed her by the washing of water with the word, so that he might present the church to himself in splendor, without spot or wrinkle or any such thing, that she might be holy and without blemish" (Eph. 5:25-27).

All of life is designed to perfect us.

A CALL TO FELLOWSHIP

The power of consecration is a call to fellowship and commune with the One that is Holy. We cannot obtain holiness without encounters with the One who is Holy.

When Jesus walked the earth, the holiness of Yahweh appeared in human form. Divine holiness became human holiness that we might see it, desire it, and ultimately partake of it.

Therefore, the call to consecration is not a call to rules and regulations, as the orphaned heart might understand it, but an invitation to encounter the person of Jesus Christ. He is the provision for the calling to live holy. Holy living is learning how live in Him.

Jesus is the plumb line.

The double-barrel shotgun of the holiness preacher is the preaching of the standard of holiness but also the empowerment to live holy according to that standard: Jesus Christ.

The only thing that gives us the right to come before a Holy God is the blood of Jesus Christ that was shed at Calvary. We cannot approach God with boldness or confidence because we have had a good day or because we feel extra spiritual. The reason we have confidence to approach His throne is because Jesus Christ took our sin upon himself. He paid the penalty for us and reconciled us to the Father. My faith in him and what he has done allows me to come and commune with God.

"Holy" and "in Christ" are perhaps the most wonderful words in the Bible.

But how powerful they become when combined: "holy in Christ."

"Holiness is not the way to Christ," says Charles Spurgeon, "Christ is the way to holiness.[2]

God's response to the question, "How can I be holy?" is "You are holy in My Son Jesus Christ."

"In Christ" is the bridge that spans the gulf between the holiness of God and humankind. In Christ, God and humankind meet.

Just as the Old Testament has no higher word than "holy," the New Testament has none deeper than "in Christ."

Being in Him, abiding in Him, being rooted in Him, growing up in Him and into Him are all divine expression of the wonderful and complete oneness between us and our Savior possible in the human heart.

When writing to the believers at Philippi in Philippians 1:1, Paul addressed his letter to "all the holy ones in Christ Jesus."

"In Christ" tells us of God's provision for our holiness. It is a revelation of what God has given us and of what we already are, of what God waits to work in us and what can be ours in personal, practical possession. "In Christ," when gratefully accepted, joyfully confessed, trustfully pleaded by sons and daughters, will be our pledge to and power of attaining holiness.

"If then you have been raised with Christ," admonishes Paul, "seek the things that are above, where Christ is, seated at the right hand of God. Set your minds on things that are above, not on things that are on earth. For you have died, and your life is hidden with Christ in God. When Christ who is your life appears, then you also will appear with him in glory."

"Put to death therefore what is earthly in you: sexual immorality, impurity, passion, evil desire, and covetousness, which is idolatry" (Col. 3:1-5).

God created five days and called them good. He created man on the sixth day and said that day was very good, but on the seventh day, when He rested, God consecrated the day and called it "Holy."

He sanctified it by taking possession of it for Himself. Where God enters and rests, there is holiness. The more perfectly the object is fitted for Him to enter and dwell, the more perfect the holiness.

Has God redeemed us? Has He rescued and delivered us from our former ways of life?

Yes!

Has He called us to holiness and consecration?

Yes!

Has He provided a way to live and be consecrated?

Yes!

Then why do so many of us live in secret sin?

Why are our lives compromised?

Where is our plumb line?

Our understanding of what it means to be redeemed is far too limited.

Our understanding of redemption must not stop at "Jesus delivered and saved me from my sin." It must move into a revelation that He redeemed me for and unto Himself—that he might have full possession of all of me!

"Flee from sexual immorality," Paul exhorts the Corinthians in First Corinthians 6:18-20. Why? Because "Every other sin a person commits is outside the body, but the sexually immoral person sins against his own body. Or do you not know that your body is a temple of the Holy Spirit within you, whom you have from God? You are not your own, for you were bought with a price. So glorify God in your body."

Perfect holiness is where God has entered in and taken complete and entire possession of a human being. It is redemption realized and filling my soul that will bring assurance and the experience of all that His power can work in me.

God has made us His own, and allows us to say that we are His, but He waits for us to yield to Him an enlarged entrance into the secret place of our inner being so that He can fill us with His fullness. Holiness is not something we bring to God or do for Him. Holiness is what there is of God in us. God has made us His own in redemption that He might make Himself our own in sanctification. Our work in becoming holy is bringing our whole life, every part of it, into subjection to the rule of our holy God, putting every member and every power upon His alter.[3]

The most precious part of the call to consecration is the yielding of ourselves to Him who has taken us as His own.

"So you also must consider yourselves dead to sin and alive to God in Christ Jesus," Paul counsels the Romans.

"Let not sin therefore reign in your mortal body, to make you obey its passions. Do not present your members to sin as instruments for unrighteousness, but present yourselves to God as those who have been brought from death to life, and your members to God as instruments for righteousness. For sin will have no dominion over you, since you are not under law but under grace" (Rom. 6:11-14). The call to consecration is the call from being a slave of sin to a son or daughter of righteousness.

A PROPHETIC WARNING

When churches/church leaders no longer confront sin in their midst, the glory of God will depart from among them and many don't even know it! If you are attending a church/ministry where sin is not being confronted on a regular basis, you are in danger of fellowshipping with Ichabod.

I fear that a spirit of Eli has come upon far too many church leaders in this hour and they are breeding a generation of Hophnis and Phinehases in the Church because of it. However, I see God raising up an army of intercessors who understand this revelation (Hannahs) and they will begin to give birth to and see the true rise of "Samuel Prophets" in our day who will call out church leaders operating in a spirit of Eli and demand repentance from a generation of Hophnis and Phinehases in the Church.

Saints, please beware of Ichabod churches, ministries, and leaders! They are easy to spot because they do not confront sin or call people to repentance and consecration. You must get out now! Their spiritual blindness and lack of anointing to stand before the Lord is going to cost you everything so long as you sit underneath their teaching and connect to their churches/ministries.

Let the Samuels arise! Let the Hannahs come forth! Let the Elis be exposed! Let Hophni and Phinehas repent! May the true GLORY OF GOD return to the Church!

NOTES

1.   R. Loren Sandford, *The Prophetic Church: Wielding the Power to Change the World,* Ada, MI: Chosen Books, 2009, p. 16.

2.   Quote was taken from this website: https://www .thekingdomcollective.com/spurgeon/sermon/2902/.

CHAPTER NINE

BREAK UP THE
FALLOW GROUND

THE CHURCH MAY CRY OUT THAT IT "WANTS A HEART that is fully in love," but the Consecrated Bride can't have a heart fully in love without giving itself to thorough heart preparation. "Sow for yourselves righteousness," Hosea exhorts us, "reap steadfast love. Break up your fallow ground, for it is time to seek the Lord, that He may come and rain righteousness on you" (10:12).

Hosea outlines three stages in the heart's renewal: (1) heart preparation, (2) prevailing prayer, and (3) spiritual revival (spiritual rain). Only out of a heart plowed deep proceeds the kind of prevailing prayer that brings true spiritual revival.

God sets this pattern in Second Chronicles 7:14 when He promises that, if those "who are called by My name will humble themselves, and pray and seek my face and turn from their wicked ways, then I will hear from heaven, will forgive their sin, and heal their land."

The pattern is the same: heart preparation is coupled with prevailing prayer and revival follows.

When most people pray for revival, they are probably asking for a wonderful experience at church at 11:00

am. Revival is more than a Sunday morning experience. When a believer prays for revival, he or she is asking God for life-shaking experiences at a personal cost. In revival, the seeker confronts sin and repents deeply. It's agonizing; it's consuming. No one has time for hobbies, for chores around the house, for work, for sleep.

Revival crashes your Daytimer, interrupts TV times, demands our full attention, and wears us out. When we pray for revival, we typically assume we are asking God to "sic 'em" on the bad guys.

Little do we realize that revival begins with us, the people of God.

Revival is divine intervention in the normal course of spiritual things. God reveals Himself to man in such awful holiness and irresistible power that human personalities are overshadowed and human programs are abandoned. Man retires to the background because God has taken the field.

Charles Finney, the Father of Modern Revivalism, describes the process of breaking up our fallow ground:

> You must remove every obstruction. Things
> may be left that you think little things, and you
> may wonder why you do not feel as you wish to
> in your walk with God, when the reason is that
> your proud and carnal mind has covered up

something which God required you to confess and remove.

Break up all the ground and turn it over. Don't *balk* it, as the farmers say; don't turn aside for little difficulties; drive the plow right through them, beam deep, and turn the ground all up, so that it may all be mellow and soft, and fit to receive the seed and bear fruit a hundred fold.[1]

The most common harbinger of revival is the prostration of convicted souls. Such heavy conviction characterized the revivals of George Whitefield and John Wesley. Lady Huntingdon wrote to Whitefield about those who were crying out and falling down at his meetings and advised him not to remove them, as he had been doing, for it dampened the meetings.

"You are making a mistake," she urged him. "Don't be wiser than God. Let them cry out; it will do a great deal more good than your preaching."

REVIVAL IS HOLINESS AND CONVICTION OF SIN

In his book *Revival: A People Saturated with God*, Brian Edwards explains that one of the most singular evidences of genuine revival is a deepening conviction of sin and a growing passion for holiness. In revival, people weep over sin and are consumed with the desire to consecrate their lives to the Lord.

"Revival is always a revival of holiness," Edwards writes, "And it begins with a terrible conviction of sin. It is often the form that this conviction of sin takes that troubles those who read of revival. Sometimes the experience is crushing. People weep uncontrollably, and worse! But there is no such thing as a revival without tears of conviction and sorrow."

This has been the testimony of the Church throughout its history. Fresh encounters with the glory of God release conviction of sin and a desire for holiness. Whenever God manifests His Presence in power and people stand before the holiness and majesty of His glory, they are undone (Isa. 6).

In the 1940s, a group of missionaries in India began praying for revival. "We began to become so desperate for revival that we read Hosea 10:12. First God showed us that our life was practically prayerless except for our routine morning and evening devotions. We became acutely aware of our need for persistent intercession. What followed was deep conviction of personal sin. One thing after another was revealed to us that had to come out and it broke our hearts."[2]

Arthur Wallis recounts the testimony of a member of a deeply devoted group praying for revival on the Isle of

Lewis in 1949. She had asked the Lord to reveal anything in her that that was hindering revival. She writes, "It was as though scales fell from my eyes and I saw my heart as I had never yet seen it. Although I had confessed all my sins to God, I had to confess something to someone I had wronged for years. I wept for hours [and] cried to God for strength to confess. After some days I confessed part, but not the whole. I had a measure of peace, but knew that God wanted absolute obedience."

At the next prayer meeting the story of Ananias and Sapphira was read, the solemn account of two who "kept back part of the price" (Acts 5). The sister was moved, but thought that God was speaking to someone else. The following night she went to bed feeling wretched. In the early hours she awoke, feeling God's hand upon her, and His holy Presence filled the room. She cried aloud, "O Lord, I can't bear it! What must I do?"

The Lord said, "Are you prepared to pay the price of revival?"

"What is the price, Lord?"

"A full confession," was the answer.

She cried out, "How can I pay it, Lord?" Afraid to live and afraid to die, she spent the night in agony of soul. The next day this sister made full confession with tears to the one concerned, feeling that had she not done so her life would be taken away.[3]

This is the testimony of the history of the Cchurch: encounters with the glory of God produce conviction of sin and a desire for holiness.

Asahel Nettleton, a trigger of America's Second Great Awakening in the 1800's, described one remarkable meeting in Schenectady, New York, in the summer of 1819:

> The room was so crowded that we were obliged to request all who had recently found relief to retire below, and spend their time in prayer for those above. This evening will never be forgotten. The scene is beyond description. Did you ever witness two hundred sinners, with one accord in one place, weeping for their sins? Until you have seen this, you have no adequate conceptions of the solemn scene. I felt as though I was standing on the verge of the eternal world while the floor under my feet was shaken by the trembling of anxious souls in view of a judgment to come. The solemnity was still heightened when every knee was bent at the throne of grace and the intervening silence of the voice of prayer was interrupted only by the sighs and sobs of anxious souls.[4]

Deep, uncomfortable, and at times an overwhelming conviction of sin is an indispensable part of revival. Too often we view revival through tinted glasses, seeing it as a time of glory and joy and swelling numbers lining up to enter churches.

That is only part of the story.

Before the glory and the joy, there is conviction and a call to holiness that begins with the people of God.

Elmer L. Towns, who co-founded Liberty University with Jerry Falwell in 1971, describes the revival that hit the university two short years later:

> When revival came to Liberty University and Thomas Road Baptist Church in the fall of 1973, glory flooded the church auditorium. It was atmospheric revival. All normal activities in our lives shut down. Students and business people didn't want to leave the sanctuary because when they left the building, they were leaving the Presence of God. They didn't want to miss anything that God was doing.
>
> Revival began on Wednesday evening about 10:30 pm, an hour after prayer meeting was over. It came when students and church members were milling around the front of the sanctuary.
>
> Most of the ushers and pastors had gone home. One student went to the pulpit—weeping—to confess sins. The microphone and pulpit lights were off, but God was there. The student's

passionate repentance captured those who were still in the auditorium.

Someone began singing.

A pianist ran to the play the piano.

People dropped to their knees beside the altar and front pews.

The piano was playing softly, not interrupting the sacred sound of tears. Shortly, another broken person approached the pulpit to confess sins. After two hours, frantic phone calls went out to the pastor and deacons:

"Revival's hit the church!"

"Church members were awakened in the middle of the night, hurriedly dressed, and drove through the dark streets of Lynchburg. All came back to the church building expecting to experience God. No ties, no Sunday morning dresses—just believers eager for the touch of God.

They stayed at the church from Wednesday until Saturday morning. Classes were canceled, most didn't leave for work, some didn't eat. When drowsiness couldn't be fought off, students slept in the pews in the back of the auditorium, some slept under the pews. Like the tide that comes and goes, there would be intense times when people were confessing their sins, then soft times of quiet weeping and private prayer around the altar.

What stopped the revival? Early Saturday morning one student rose to confess his sins, but he seemed to be bragging about what he did when he sinned; there was no shame nor brokenness. The Holy Spirit—who knows the heart—departed the meeting. Within one hour, all knew the revival was over. All left, went home and went back about their daily activities."[5]

Francis Chan puts it like this:

The benchmark of success in church services has become more about attendance than the movement of the Holy Spirit. The entertainment model of church was largely adopted in the 80's and 90's and while it alleviated boredom for a few hours a week, it filled our churches with self-focused consumers rather than self-sacrificing servants of Jesus Christ.[6]

The entertainment model of the Church is creating meetings where people are taught how to function at services—how to serve—when they should be learning how to move in the power of the Spirit and encounter Jesus.

HEARTS MUST BE PREPARED
FOR ENCOUNTER

Fallow ground is ground that has yielded fruit in the past but is currently largely unproductive through the lack of cultivation. It is land lying idle. Seed may be sown on it, the heavens might send rain, but neither the seed nor the rain will produce much life because of its uncultivated state. This lack of cultivation gives that fallow ground three characteristics: it is hard, it is weed covered, and it is unfruitful.

1.   Fallow ground is hard. Hardness comes when our hearts are insensitive to sins that grieve the Holy Spirit. The sins that produce the greatest hardness often emerge out of the orphan spirit: bitterness, resentment, unforgiveness, anger, gossip, slander, pride. Our orphaned hearts grow cold and hardened toward the people of God and we don't care about lost souls dying and going to hell.

In this state, believers may diligently listen to the ministry of God's Word and be in a service where God is present, but their lives never change. The soil of their heart is hardened by the heart's sinful attitudes and has never been plowed.

2.   Fallow ground is weed covered. The reason farmers cultivate fields is to eliminate weeds that overrun good seed or growing plants and stunt their growth or kill

them. Jeremiah warned Israel to "Break up your fallow ground and sow not among the thorns" (4:3).

When we do not diligently cultivate our hearts, thorns and weeds abound.

It is time to cease excusing our sins by calling them shortcomings or by blaming them on the actions and injustices of other people. It's time to cease justifying our carnal thinking and materialistic ways by pointing at everyone else and finding comfort in comparisons.

That is orphan thinking.

We must not deal lightly with our sins.

3. Fallow ground is unfruitful. The fruit God expects and desires is not more religious activity, not greater service, but Christlike character: sons and daughters displaying their Father's image! This is fruit of the Spirit: love, joy, peace, patience, kindness, goodness, faithfulness, gentleness, self-control.

Describing the scriptural principles of revival he witnessed in action during the Hebrides Revival in Scotland from 1948 to 1952, Arthur Wallis writes:

> If Hosea's figure of fallow ground is an accurate description of our own hearts, and if we are deeply concerned to remedy the situation, then we must face this command: "Break up your fallow ground."

There is a sense in which God may break us in order to bless us, but here God places the onus upon us by commanding us to do it. It is as dangerous to expect God, by some sovereign act, to do for us what He has commanded us to do for ourselves as it is to strive to do for ourselves what He has promised to do for us.

In the path of spiritual progress, there is no little emphasis in Scripture on that part the believer has to play. We read, "Cleanse your hands, ye sinners; and purify your hearts, ye doubleminded" (James 4:8), and again "Let us cleanse ourselves from all defilement of flesh and spirit, perfecting holiness in the fear of God' (2 Cor. 7:1). Thus it is with this question of heart preparation: the responsibility is ours.

This is not only true in... revival, but in all Christian service and witness: "The preparations of the heart belong to man: but the answer of the tongue is from the Lord" (Prov. 16:1).

So there is our part and God's part. If we make it our business to have prepared hearts, God will make it His business to fill our mouths with arguments which our adversaries shall not be able to gainsay or resist. "Sanctify in your hearts Christ as Lord," says Peter, and you will be "ready always to give answer to every man that asketh you a reason concerning the hope that is in you" (1 Pet. 3:15).

God's contention with Israel was that they were "a stubborn and rebellious generation, a generation that prepared not their heart" (Ps. 78:8)

If we are to have revival, it must come from heaven, it must be the result of divine intervention; but how can we expect God to rain righteousness upon us before we have broken up the fallow ground? The words of Samuel should come as a challenge to the people of God today: "Prepare your hearts unto the Lord, and serve him only, and He will deliver you out of the hand of the Philistines" (I Sam. 7:3).

Are you ready to obey?

To "break up the fallow ground" of our hearts means to bring them to a humble and contrite state before God, for this is the only state of heart that God can revive, the only state that is ready for the rain of revival. "For thus saith the high and lofty One that inhabiteth eternity, whose name is Holy: I dwell in the high and holy place, with him also that is of a contrite and humble spirit, to revive the spirit of the humble and to revive the heart of the contrite ones" (Isa. 57:15).[7]

This overwhelming sense of encounter with God bringing deep conviction of sin is perhaps the most outstanding feature of true revival.

Charles Finney, preaching in the village schoolhouse near Antwerp, New York, in the midst of America's Second Great Awakening, described the results of encounter like this: "An awful solemnity seemed to settle down upon [the people]; the congregation began to fall from their seats in every direction, and cried for mercy. If I had had a sword in each hand, I could not have cut them off their seats as fast as they fell... I was obliged to stop preaching."[8]

Wallis describes the great revival of Ulster, Ireland, claimed to have made the greatest spiritual impact on Ireland since St Patrick:

> No town in Ulster was more deeply stirred during the 1859 revival than Coleraine. It was there that a boy was so troubled about his soul that the schoolmaster sent him home. An older boy, a Christian, accompanied him, and before they had gone far led him to Christ.
>
> "Returning at once to the school, this latest convert testified to the master, "Oh, I am so happy! I have the Lord Jesus in my heart."
>
> The effect of these artless words was very great. Boy after boy rose and silently left the room. On investigation the master found these boys

ranged alongside the wall of the playground, every one apart and on his knees! Very soon their silent prayer became a bitter cry. It was heard by those within and pierced their hearts.

They cast themselves upon their knees, and their cry for mercy was heard in the girls' school-room above. In a few moments the whole school was upon its knees, and its wail of distress was heard in the street outside. Neighbors and pass-ersby came flocking in, and all, as they crossed the threshold, came under the same convicting power. Every room was filled with men, women, and children seeking God.[9]

When men and women are made aware of the fresh Presence of Jesus in their midst, they become aware of the sin hiding within them. "The ruthless logic of Jonathan Edwards's famous discourse, 'Sinners in the Hands of an Angry God,' preached in his usual plain and unde-monstrative manner in 1741 at Enfield, Connecticut, could never have produced the effect it did had not God been in the midst. When they went into the meeting-house, the appearance of the assembly was thoughtless and vain. The people hardly conducted themselves with common decency."[10]

The effect of the sermon changed this scene instantly. "The assembly appeared...bowed down, with an awful conviction of their sin and danger. There was such a breathing of distress, and weeping, that the preacher was obliged to speak to the people and desire silence, that he might be heard," one observer records.[11]

Another described the congregation this way: "Many of the hearers were seen unconsciously holding themselves up against the pillars, and the sides of the pews, as though they already felt themselves sliding into the pit."[12]

"Search me, O God, and know my heart," cries David in Psalm 139. "Try me and know my anxious thoughts; See if there is any offensive way in me and lead me in Thy way everlasting!"

God-consciousness characterized David's life. Encounter had prepared his heart for a spirit of wisdom and revelation in the knowledge of who God is.

"Behold, you desire truth in the inward parts!" he cries out in Psalm 51, under heavy conviction for his sin with Bathsheba.

"Who can ascend to the hill of the Lord?" he asks in Psalm 24, "Who may stand in His holy place?"

His answer? "The one who has clean hands and a pure heart, who does not trust in an idol or swear by what is false."

How do we break up the fallow ground?

Perhaps Joel says it best: "Rend your heart, not your garments. Return to the Lord!"

NOTES

1. Charles Finney, "Break Up Your Fallow Ground," *The Independent*, New York: The Independent of New York, 5 February 1874.

2. Missionaries Seeking Revival in India, 1940.

3. Arthur Wallis, *In the Day of Thy Power: The Spiritual Principles of Revival*, London: Christian Literature Crusade, 2010, pp. 122–123.

4. William Francis Pringle Noble, *A Century of Gospel-work: A History of the Growth of Evangelical Religion in the United States*, Philadelphia: H. C. Watts and Company, 1876, p. 295.

5. Elmer L. Towns and Douglas Porter, *The Ten Greatest Revivals Ever: From Pentecost to the Present*. Shippensburg, PA: Destiny Image, 2000, p. 79-80.

6. Francis Chan, *Forgotten God: Reversing our Tragic Neglect of the Holy Spirit*, Elgin, IL: David C. Cook, 2010, p. 90.

7. Arthur Wallis, *In the Day of Thy Power: The Spiritual Principles of Revival*, London: Christian Literature Crusade, 2010, pp. 115-116.

8. Charles Finney, *Memoirs of Charles Finney*, p. 103.

9. Arthur Wallis, *In the Day of Thy Power: The Spiritual Principles of Revival*, London: Christian Literature Crusade, 2010, p. 77.

10. Ibid.

11. Ibid.
12. Ibid.

CHAPTER TEN

SPIRITUAL
BANKRUPTCY

ONE OF THE SECRETS THAT THE CONSECRATED BRIDE will treasure in her heart is the power of being in tune with how much She needs the Bridegroom. Her ability to glory in her own spiritual bankruptcy will invite the romance and fragrance of her King like never before.

What would you say to someone who asked if Jesus is a crutch for people who can't make it on their own?

If Jesus is a crutch, then He's only good for paralyzed cripples.

But we don't like to see ourselves as cripples, do we?

It's offensive to our self-sufficiency to confess that without Jesus, we are nothing.

Ralph Waldo Emerson, American poet and philosopher, wrote a famous essay called "Self-reliance," capturing the spirit of our age: "Trust thyself: every heart vibrates to that iron string."

Emerson's words stand in stark contrast with the words of Jesus: "I do nothing on my own initiative" (John 5:30).

Jesus Christ is a stumbling block not only to Ralph Waldo Emerson but to you and I at times because He takes the disease that we most hate, helplessness, and instead of curing it, makes it the entrance to the Kingdom of heaven.

Confessing our absolute helplessness without Him to the Lord attracts His fire! It invites our Bridegroom King to come to our rescue and work His strength and power within us and through us!

Paul unashamedly declared "Not that we are adequate in ourselves as considering anything coming from ourselves, but our adequacy is from God" (2 Cor. 3:5). In Philippians 3:3 he says again, "I glory in Jesus Christ and put no confidence in the flesh!" Jesus Himself declared to His disciples "Apart from me, you can do nothing" (John 15:5).

Do Not Trust the Flesh

Real revival falls on communities of people who daily confess how much they need the grace of God. The Consecrated Bride will live a lifestyle of utter dependency and trust in Christ alone. Listen to the words of Jeremiah the prophet as he declares, "Let not the wise man boast in his wisdom, let not the mighty man boast in his might, let not the rich man boast in his riches, but let him who boasts boast in this, that he understands and knows me, that I am the Lord who practices steadfast love, justice, and righteousness in the earth. For in these things I delight," declares the Lord (Jer. 9:23-24).

Later in Jeremiah, the Lord warns again, "Cursed is the man who trusts in man and makes flesh his strength, whose heart turns away from the Lord. He is like a shrub in the desert, and shall not see any good come. He shall dwell in the parched places of the wilderness, in an uninhabited salt land" (17:5-6).

The Danger of Spiritual Pride

One of the primary obstacles to embracing our spiritual bankruptcy or helplessness in our walk with Christ is our pride. Unfortunately, the longer some of us walk with Christ, the more we think we have got it down. We have heard it all, read it, seen it, and we deceive ourselves into believing that we are spiritually mature.

Jesus says to the church of Laodicea: "I know your works: you are neither cold nor hot. Would that you were either cold or hot! So, because you are lukewarm, and neither hot nor cold, I will spit you out of my mouth. For you say, I am rich, I have prospered, *and I need nothing*, not realizing that you are wretched, pitiable, poor, blind, and naked" (Rev. 3:14-17).

It is not the spiritually mature that have need of nothing; it is actually the lukewarm! Jesus Christ is going to spit the Harlot Bride out of His mouth who have been deceived into believing they do not have to confess their great need of Him. "In their own eyes they flatter themselves too much to detect or hate their sin," David says in Psalm 36:2.

THE SERMON ON THE MOUNT

It is no coincidence that Jesus Christ therefore chose to list spiritual bankruptcy as the first beatitude in the Sermon on the Mount in Matthew 5:1-11. Kenneth Wuest, a Greek scholar translates the first eleven verses of Matthew 5 like this:

> And when he had seated himself, his pupils came to him. And having opened his mouth, he went to teaching them, saying, "Spiritually prosperous are the destitute and helpless in the realm of the spirit (spiritual bankruptcy) because theirs is the kingdom of heaven.
>
> Spiritually prosperous are those who are mourning because they themselves shall be encouraged and strengthened by consolation.
>
> Spiritually prosperous are those who are meek because they themselves shall inherit the earth.
>
> Spiritually prosperous are those hungering and thirsting for righteousness because they themselves shall be filled so as to be completely satisfied.

Spiritually prosperous are those who are merciful because they themselves shall be the objects of mercy.

Spiritually prosperous are those who are pure in the sphere of the heart because they themselves shall see God.

Spiritually prosperous are those who make peace because they themselves shall be called sons of God.

Spiritually prosperous are those who have been persecuted on account of righteousness because theirs is the kingdom of heaven."

Spiritually prosperous are you whenever they shall revile you and persecute you and say every pernicious thing against you, speaking deliberate falsehoods on account of me. Be rejoicing and exult exceedingly because your reward is great in heaven. For in this manner they persecuted the prophets who were before you.[1]

What is your definition of spiritual prosperity? Imagine the description of a mature believer in the eyes of Jesus Christ. This person is destitute and helpless in the realm of the Spirit. In other words Jesus is saying, "My Consecrated Bride will confess her spiritual bankruptcy apart from Me and I will pour out My blessings and Holy Spirit because of her humility!"

THE TRUTH

The honest truth is that are all destitute and helpless in the realm of the Spirit whether we know it or not, but the true blessing is found in willingly confessing our spiritual bankruptcy.

Spiritual prosperity begins with seeing we are destitute and helpless (being poor in spirit). It increases when we feel this destitution and helplessness as well as see it and we mourn (the second beatitude). Awareness of our lack before people produces meekness (the third beatitude). Others know it, too. Then we hunger and thirst for the righteousness. We lack and He fills us!

THE FIRST PRINCIPLE OF THE KINGDOM

Oswald Chambers calls the first beatitude in Matthew 5:1-12 "the first principle of the Kingdom." He goes on to warn, "As long as we have a conceited, self-righteous idea that we can do things how we want to do them, God has to allow us to go on until we break the neck of our ignorance over some obstacle. Then we will be willing to come and receive from Him."

"The bed-rock of Jesus Christ's Kingdom is poverty, not possession; not decisions for Jesus Christ, but a sense of absolute futility. "I cannot go on without You!"

"Then," says Jesus, "Blessed are you."

"That is the entrance, and it takes us a long while to believe we are poor. The knowledge of our own poverty brings us to the moral frontier where Jesus Christ works."[2]

Charles Price explains "poor in spirit" as the "first step to real happiness... an acknowledgement of spiritual poverty, the recognition of the fact I do not have in myself what it takes to be the person I was created to be. This is deeper than recognizing I fail. It is realizing I do not have the capacity within myself to do anything else!"

> As Paul wrote, "I know that nothing good lives in me, that is, in my sinful nature" (more literally, "in my natural self") (Rom. 7:18). David wrote, "I said to the Lord, You are my Lord; apart from you I have no good thing" (Ps. 16:2). When Paul says, "nothing good lives in me," it is not that everything about him is bad! Elsewhere he lists some things about which he says he could boast, but he is saying that apart from the indwelling Presence of Jesus Christ, everything else which may be good about me is ultimately good for nothing. I am like a car without an engine.

> It is to face this fact and acknowledge our own poverty of spirit, which is the first step to real happiness. It is to this person Jesus says, "the kingdom of heaven is theirs." All the riches of the kingdom of heaven are available to the

person who recognizes their own bankruptcy without God.[3]

BLESSED ARE THE
SPIRITUALLY BANKRUPT

For Bible commentator J. C. Ryle, "the poor in spirit" are the "humble and lowly-minded and self-abased... those who are deeply convinced of their own sinfulness in God's sight. These are people who are not 'wise in their own eyes and clever in their own sight' (Is. 5:21). They are not 'rich, blind, and naked' (Rev. 3:17). Blessed are all such. Humility is the very first letter in the alphabet of Christianity. We must begin low, if we want to build high."[4]

Martin Lloyd-Jones says that "poor in spirit" is "ultimately a man's attitude toward himself... This is something which is not only not admired by the world; it is despised by it. You will never find a greater antithesis to the worldly spirit and outlook than that which you find in this verse. What emphasis the world places on its belief in self-reliance, self-confidence, and self-expression!"

Lloyd-Jones continues: "The Sermon on the Mount, in other words, comes to us and says, 'There is the mountain that you have to scale, the heights you have to climb, and the first thing you must realize, as you look at that mountain which you are told you must ascend, is that you cannot do it, that you are utterly incapable in and of yourself, and that any attempt to do it in your own strength is proof positive that you have not understood it."[5]

THE LITMUS TEST

The litmus test of whether we are in tune with our own spiritual bankruptcy is discovered in whether or not we have a prayer life. Nothing says, "I need you God" more than a life lived down on our knees. People that are out of touch with their need for God do not pray because they have become their own god. There are even many churches and individuals who started their walked with God dependent upon Him but Paul warns the Galatians, "Are you so foolish?" Paul cries out to the Galatians, "Having begun by the Spirit, are you now being perfected by the flesh?" (3:3).

A SPIRITUALLY BANKRUPT BELIEVER

An incredible example of a man who truly confessed and lived a lifestyle of spiritual bankruptcy before God was William Carey, known as the Father of Modern Missions. Listen to this story of his life and allow the Holy Spirit to minister to your heart.

> When the fire of 1812 destroyed dozens of his precious manuscripts, William Carey didn't blame the devil. He said, "How unsearchable are the ways of God!"

And then he accused himself of too much self-congratulation in his labors and said, "The Lord has smitten us, he had a right do to so, and we deserve His corrections.'"

When he had outlived four of his comrades in mission, he wrote back to Andrew Fuller, "I know not why so fruitless a tree is preserved; but the Lord is too wise to err."

When he died in 1834 in Serampore, India, a simple tablet was put on his grave with the words he requested. And when you hear these I want you to ask: What was William Carey's secret?

How could he persevere for forty years over all obstacles—as a homely man, suffering from recurrent fever, limping for years from an injury in 1817, and yet putting the entire Bible into six languages and parts of it into 29 other languages—what was the secret of this man's usefulness and productivity for the kingdom?

The tablet on his grave reads:

WILLIAM CAREY

Born August 17the, 1761

Died June 9the, 1834

A wretched, poor, and helpless worm,

On Thy kind arms I fall.

His secret was in the last line of his epitaph: "On Thy kind arms I fall." This was his secret in dying and this was his secret in living. He cast himself—poor, helpless, despicable—on the kind arms of God, for he knew the promise of Jesus: "Blessed are the poor in spirit, for to them belong the merciful and mighty arms of the King of Kings."[6]

CALL ON HIS NAME TODAY!

The Bible says that the ungodly are those who "do not call on the Lord" (Ps. 14:4). The ungodly will do many things, but they continually refuse to humble themselves and recognize God's greatness by calling on His name. Salvation itself is impossible until a person humbly calls upon the name of the Lord (Acts 2:21), for God has promised specifically to be rich in mercy to those who call on His name (Rom. 10:12-13).

We must understand that one of Satan's main strategies toward humanity has always been to whisper, "Don't call, don't ask, don't depend on God for anything. Just rely on your own strengths and abilities and you will be fine."

These statements are all demonic lies that must be exposed and removed from our thinking!

In contrast, listen to David's confident words in Psalm 4:3 as he says, "Know that the Lord has set apart the

GODLY for Himself; the Lord WILL HEAR WHEN I CALL TO HIM."

The ungodly do not call upon God and He does not hear them, but the godly call upon Him and He answers them!

Are we calling upon God in the place of prayer and therefore bearing the fruit of godly living or are we neglecting Him and demonstrating ungodly living by refusing to humble ourselves and confess our great need for Him? The Consecrated Bride is going to rise in the earth and confidently and triumphantly call upon the Bridegroom as their ultimate source of joy, satisfaction, and deliverance from themselves. Oh, what a glorious cry it will be!

NOTES

1. Kenneth S. Wuest, *The New Testament: An Expanded Translation.*

2. Oswald Chambers, *Studies in the Sermon on the Moun,* Hants UK: Marshall, Morgan & Scott.

3. Charles Price, *Focus on the Bible: Matthew.*

4. J. C. Ryle, *Matthew.*

5. Martin Lloyd-Jones, *Studies in the Sermon on the Mount.*

6. John Piper, "Blessed are the Poor in Spirit Who Mourn," Desiring God, 2 February 1986.

THE FULL PRETERIST WARNING

I FELT STRONGLY URGED BY THE HOLY SPIRIT TO WARN the Consecrated Bride that a great deception is currently sweeping and will in the days ahead attempt to sweep large portions of the Church, and the alarm must be sounded! It's called "full preterism" and it's currently being specifically pushed by some so-called "apostles."

Full preterism is the belief that the prophecies in Matthew 24 (spoken by Jesus on the Mount of Olives) and the Book of Revelation were completely fulfilled in the PAST, particularly in the events leading up to and surrounding the destruction of Jerusalem by the Romans in A.D. 70. According to Full Preterists,

- The Tribulation

- The Antichrist

- The Abomination of Desolation

- Jesus's Second Coming (Matthew 24; Revelation 19)

are all things of the past.

Here are five prophetic warnings God has given me for those potentially being deceived into this dangerous doctrine by "apostles."

FULL PRETERISM OPERATES IN A SCOFFING SPIRIT

In Second Peter 3:3-4, Peter is emphatic: "Most importantly, I want to remind you that in the last days SCOFFERS will come, MOCKING the truth and following their own desires. They will say, 'What happened to the promise that Jesus is coming again?'

A scoffing and mocking spirit operates in some circles in the body of Christ toward the return of Jesus Christ. They believe He has already come and any tribulation or persecution is not a future event. You will hear full preterists constantly mock and scoff at references to the "end times" as they glory in their deception.

FULL PRETERISM LEADS TO HYPER GRACE THEOLOGY

The apostles in the New Testament constantly appealed to the second coming of Jesus as a primary reason for why the Church must live holy and righteously before God.

Paul prays in First Thessalonians 3:13 that God might strengthen believers' hearts so that they "will be blameless and holy in the presence of our God and Father when our Lord Jesus comes with all his holy ones."

Again, Paul charges believers in First Timothy 6:13 "to keep this command without spot or blame until the appearing of our Lord Jesus Christ, which God will bring about in his own time."

And in Titus 2:12-14, Paul admonishes believers that "Grace teaches us to say 'No' to ungodliness and worldly passions, and to live self—controlled, upright and godly lives in this present age, while we wait for the blessed hope—the glorious appearing of our great God and Savior, Jesus Christ, who gave himself for us to redeem us from all wickedness and to purify for himself a people that are his very own, eager to do what is good."

Holiness and consecration are rarely if at all emphasized and preached among full preterists. They typically embrace hyper grace theology and never appeal to the return of Jesus Christ as to why people should be living right with God. Many of them will claim that we are living in a "better covenant" and God is no longer judging anyone.

Full Preterism Breeds Lazy and Complacent Christianity

The urgency of the hour and the fact that Jesus Christ could return at any moment fueled the zeal and passion of the first-century Church for the proclamation of the gospel message and the repentance of sin. John urges believers as "dear children" to "continue in him, so that when he appears we may be confident and unashamed before him at his coming" (1 John 2:28).

Peter warns in Acts 3:19-21, "Repent, then, and turn to God, so that your sins may be wiped out, that times of refreshing may come from the Lord, and that he may send the Christ, who has been appointed for you—even Jesus. He must remain in heaven until the time comes for God to restore everything, as he promised long ago through his holy prophets."

Because full preterists believe that Jesus has already returned, there is no urgency for the proclamation of the Gospel or for anyone to repent of sin with fervency and sobriety.

FULL PRETERISM LEAVES THE CHURCH COMPLETELY UNPREPARED FOR THE DAYS AHEAD

Those who are deceived by full preterism will become offended and fall away as persecution and tribulations increase in many parts of the earth in the days ahead. The New Testament clearly helps believers realize that trouble will come, but in the midst of trouble, we are anchored to the promise of Jesus's bodily return. Full preterism teaches that trouble is not coming and Jesus has already returned. Therefore, there is no preparation for trouble, nor any hope in the midst of it when it comes.

Peter is clear: "But the day of the Lord will come like a thief, in which the heavens will pass away with a roar and the elements will be destroyed with intense heat, and the earth and its works will be burned up. Since all these things are to be destroyed in this way, what sort of people ought you to be in holy conduct and godliness, looking for and hastening the coming of the day of God, because of which the heavens will be destroyed by burning, and the elements will melt with intense heat! But according to His promise we are looking for new heavens and a new earth, in which righteousness dwells" (2 Pet. 3:10-13).

FULL PRETERISM DISCONNECTS THE CHURCH FROM THE CRISIS COMING TO ISRAEL

Scripture consistently teaches that trouble will come to Jerusalem and the national salvation of all of Israel will take place. This is why we must understand this trouble and what God's plan is for it (Matt. 24:15). Full Preterism tells us all these prophecies have already been fulfilled and therefore the trouble in the Middle East has no biblical significance whatsoever.

Because full preterism does not accurately interpret the signs of our times, it creates a culture of prayerlessness, a scoffing spirit, hyper grace theology, lazy and

complacent Christianity, and a misunderstanding surrounding events in/around Israel.

Saints, beware of so-called "apostles" pushing this
belief system in the days ahead. Those who are deceived
will be given over to strong delusion! Remember, neither the apostles nor the early church fathers (leaders
of the Church in the first three centuries A.D. following
the original apostles, such as Clement of Rome, Ignatius
of Antioch, Polycarp of Smyrna, Justin Martyr, or Ter-
tullian) referenced Christ's Second Coming as having
already occurred.

COME LORD JESUS

May the Consecrated Bride continue to cultivate deep
intimacy with the Bridegroom King and be on the alert
for end time deception coming from the Harlot Bride.
The friends of the Bridegroom must continue to drop a
plumb line, a clear standard of righteousness in the land
and allow the fallow ground in their hearts to be broken
up. The Consecrated Bride must remain humble and daily
confessing Her great need for God. Though there will be a
great falling away, there will also be a tremendous revival
where the Consecrated Bride without spot or wrinkle will
rise on the Wedding Day to dine at the table of encounter
and rule and reign with the Bridegroom King forever. Let
the days we now live in be given to preparation for that

glorious day and may hearts filled with lovesickness cry out, "Maranatha! Come Lord Jesus!" (Rev. 22:20)

ABOUT
JEREMIAH JOHNSON

Jeremiah Johnson planted and is the overseer of Heart of the Father Ministry in Lakeland, Florida. A gifted teacher, prophet, and author of multiple books, Jeremiah travels extensively throughout the United States and abroad as a conference and guest speaker. He has been a guest on Christian television and radio shows including *The Jim Bakker Show*, Sid Roth's *It's Supernatural!*, and *The Line of Fire* with Dr. Michael Brown, as well as on networks such as Daystar, TBN, and God TV. Jeremiah is also the founder and director of Maranatha School of Ministry. MSM is a full-time, five-fold ministry training center that equips and sends out end-time messengers. For more information, please visit jeremiahjohnson.tv or www.maranatha.school. Jeremiah and his wife, Morgan, reside in Florida with their four children.